chapter 1: "The Suffocating Feeling of Being Stuck in a Financial Fog."

The Art of Budgeting: Your Money, Your Power

Embarking on the journey to financial empowerment begins with understanding the profound impact of budgeting. Let's delve into the key aspects that make budgeting a transformative tool:

chapter 1: The Suffocating Feeling of Being Stuck in a Financial Fog

Financial ambiguity often leads to stress and anxiety, significantly impacting mental health and overall well-being. The American Psychological Association identifies financial stress as a prevalent source of anxiety, affecting individuals' mental health.

Examples Illustrating the Impact of Financial Anxiety on Mental Health

1. Increased Psychological Distress:
   - Example: A study found that individuals with greater financial worries exhibited higher levels of psychological distress, including symptoms of anxiety and depression.

2. Development of Maladaptive Coping Mechanisms:
   - Example: Some individuals may turn to compulsive behaviors, such as excessive spending or gambling, as a way to cope with financial stress, leading to further financial strain and mental health challenges.

1. The Psychological Impact of Financial Uncertainty

Financial ambiguity often leads to stress and anxiety, affecting mental health and overall well-being. The American Psychological Association reports that financial stress is a common source of anxiety, impacting individuals' mental health.

Example 1: Consider Jane, who avoids checking her bank statements due to fear of what she might find. This avoidance increases her anxiety, leading to sleepless nights and difficulty concentrating at work.

Example 2: Mark constantly worries about unexpected expenses because he lacks a clear understanding of his financial situation. This uncertainty causes chronic stress, affecting his relationships and overall happiness.

Summary: These examples illustrate how financial uncertainty can lead to significant psychological distress, emphasizing the importance of financial clarity for mental well-being.

2. The Cycle of Overspending and Debt Accumulation

Without clear financial awareness, individuals may overspend, leading to debt accumulation and a cycle that's hard to break. Psychology Today notes that overspending can be a coping mechanism for emotional distress, complicating financial situations.

Example 1: John uses shopping as a stress reliever, unaware of his spending limits. This behavior results in mounting credit card debt, causing further financial strain.

Example 2: Lisa frequently dines out without tracking her expenses, leading to overdraft fees and increased debt. Her lack of financial oversight perpetuates a cycle of overspending and borrowing.

Summary: These scenarios demonstrate how unmonitored spending can lead to debt accumulation, highlighting the necessity of financial awareness to prevent such cycles.

3. The Importance of Tracking Expenses

Monitoring expenses is crucial for financial clarity. By tracking spending, individuals can identify patterns and make informed decisions. Investopedia emphasizes the importance of tracking expenses to prevent financial crises.

Example 1: Sarah starts using a budgeting app to log her daily expenses. She discovers she's spending more on dining out than she realized, prompting her to adjust her habits.

Example 2: Tom keeps a spreadsheet of his monthly bills and purchases. This practice helps him identify unnecessary subscriptions he can cancel to save money.

Summary: These examples show that tracking expenses can reveal spending habits, enabling individuals to make adjustments that improve their financial health.

4. Creating a Realistic Budget

Developing a budget that reflects income and expenses helps manage finances effectively. The 50/30/20 rule is a popular budgeting method that allocates income to needs, wants, and savings.

Example 1: Michael allocates 50% of his income to necessities, 30% to discretionary spending, and 20% to savings, ensuring all areas are covered.

Example 2: Emma creates a zero-based budget, assigning every dollar a purpose, which helps her control her spending and increase her savings.

Summary: These cases illustrate that creating a structured budget can provide financial direction and control, aiding in effective money management.

5. Setting Financial Goals

Establishing clear financial goals provides direction and motivation. Goals can range from short-term objectives like building an emergency fund to long-term plans like retirement savings.

Example 1: Emily sets a goal to save $5,000 for an emergency fund within a year, motivating her to cut unnecessary expenses.

Example 2: James aims to pay off his student loans in five years by making extra payments, guiding his budgeting decisions.

Summary: These examples demonstrate that setting specific financial goals can inspire disciplined financial behavior and strategic planning.

6. Seeking Professional Guidance

Consulting financial advisors or counselors can provide personalized strategies for managing finances. Professional guidance can help navigate complex financial situations and develop effective plans.

Example 1: David consults a financial advisor to create a debt repayment plan, helping him reduce his liabilities systematically.

Example 2: Laura attends financial counseling to learn about investment options, enabling her to make informed decisions about her retirement savings.

Summary: These scenarios highlight the benefits of seeking professional advice to tailor financial strategies to individual needs.

7. Building an Emergency Fund

An emergency fund acts as a financial safety net for unexpected expenses. Having such a fund can prevent reliance on credit and reduce financial stress.

Example 1: Anna saves three months' worth of living expenses, which helps her cover medical bills without incurring debt.

Example 2: Brian's emergency fund allows him to manage car repairs without disrupting his regular budget.

Summary: These examples show that an emergency fund provides financial resilience, enabling individuals to handle unforeseen costs comfortably.

8. Reducing Unnecessary Expenses

Identifying and cutting unnecessary expenses can free up resources for savings or debt repayment. This practice enhances financial efficiency.

Example 1: Sophia cancels unused gym memberships and streaming services, redirecting that money to her savings account.

Example 2: Ethan prepares meals at home instead of eating out, significantly reducing his monthly food expenses.

Summary: These cases illustrate that eliminating non-essential spending can improve financial health and support other financial goals.

9. Automating Savings

Setting up automatic transfers to savings accounts ensures consistent saving habits and reduces the temptation to overspend.

Example 1: Olivia arranges for 10% of her paycheck to be deposited directly into her savings account each month.

Example 2: Liam sets up automatic contributions to his retirement fund, ensuring regular investment without manual intervention.

Summary: These examples demonstrate that automating savings can instill discipline and facilitate the growth of financial reserves.

10. Educating Oneself Financially

Improving financial literacy empowers individuals to

Interactive Questions and Sample Answers

1. How often do you review your bank statements?

  Sample Answer: "I review my bank statements monthly to ensure I understand my spending patterns."

2. Do you track your daily expenses? If so, how?

  Sample Answer*: "Yes, I use a budgeting app to log all my daily expenses."

3. Have you set financial goals for yourself? What are they?

  Sample Answer: "Yes, my goals include paying off my credit card debt within a year and saving for a vacation."

4. Do you feel anxious when thinking about your finances?

  Sample Answer: "Sometimes, especially when unexpected expenses arise."

5. How do you plan your monthly budget?

  Sample Answer: "I allocate funds for essentials first, then distribute the remaining amount towards savings and discretionary spending."

6. Have you ever sought financial advice?

  Sample Answer: "Yes, I consulted a financial advisor to help me create a debt repayment plan."

7. Do you use credit cards for daily purchases?

Sample Answer: "Occasionally, but I try to use cash or debit to avoid accumulating debt."

8. How do you handle unexpected expenses?

Sample Answer: "I have an emergency fund that I dip into for unforeseen costs."

9. Do you compare your spending habits to others?

Sample Answer: "I try not to, as I focus on my financial goals and limitations."

10. What steps have you taken to improve your financial literacy?

Sample Answer: "I've attended workshops and read books on personal finance to better manage my money."

By addressing these questions, individuals can gain insight into their financial habits and take steps towards achieving financial clarity and stability.

These examples demonstrate how financial anxiety can lead to significant mental health challenges, including increased psychological distress and the development of maladaptive coping mechanisms. Addressing financial stress is crucial for maintaining mental well-being and preventing the escalation of mental health issues.

1. Develop a Comprehensive Budget

Creating a detailed budget allows you to track income and expenses, providing clarity on your financial situation. This awareness reduces uncertainty and helps identify areas for potential savings.

Example 1: Use a budgeting app like Mint to categorize expenses into needs, wants, and savings. For instance, allocate $1,500 for essentials like rent and utilities, $500 for discretionary spending, and $500 for savings.

Example 2: Manually create a spreadsheet to list every expense from the past month. Realize that $200 on coffee could be reduced to $50 by brewing at home, freeing $150 for debt repayment.

Summary: From these examples, you learn that budgeting isn't about restriction but about intentional allocation. Tracking every dollar fosters awareness and control, crucial for reducing financial anxiety.

2. Build an Emergency Fund

Having a financial cushion for unexpected expenses can prevent reliance on credit and significantly reduce stress.

Example 1: A freelancer saves 10% of each project payment into a high-yield savings account. After six months, they have $3,000, covering three months' living expenses.

Example 2: A teacher uses an auto-transfer system to save $200 from each paycheck. After one year, they have $2,400 set aside for emergencies like car repairs or medical bills.

Summary: These scenarios highlight that consistent, small contributions to an emergency fund can provide a sense of security and lessen anxiety about the unexpected.

3. Seek Professional Guidance

Consulting financial advisors or counselors can provide tailored strategies for managing finances and reducing anxiety.

Example 1: A financial counselor helps a young couple prioritize debt repayment, using the snowball method to pay off smaller debts first. They feel empowered as debts decrease.

Example 2: An advisor guides a mid-career professional in diversifying their investments, offering reassurance during market fluctuations by aligning investments with long-term goals.

Summary: These examples emphasize the value of seeking expert guidance for personalized financial solutions, fostering confidence and reducing stress.

4. Practice Mindfulness and Stress-Reduction Techniques

Engaging in mindfulness practices, such as meditation or deep breathing exercises, can alleviate the physical and mental effects of financial anxiety.

Example 1: A stressed entrepreneur practices 10 minutes of meditation daily, helping them approach financial decisions with clarity rather than fear.

Example 2: A recent graduate uses guided breathing exercises before reviewing student loan balances, calming their mind and enabling constructive action.

Summary: Mindfulness techniques empower individuals to manage emotional responses to financial stress, creating space for rational decision-making.

5. Educate Yourself on Personal Finance

Increasing financial literacy empowers you to make informed decisions, reducing uncertainty and associated anxiety.

Example 1: A parent attends a free budgeting workshop and learns how to cut monthly expenses by $400 through meal prepping and reducing subscriptions.

Example 2: A college student watches videos about investing basics, opening a Roth IRA and contributing $50 monthly, building confidence in long-term financial planning.

Summary: Educating yourself transforms confusion into clarity, enabling proactive financial decisions and minimizing stress.

6. Set Realistic Financial Goals

Setting achievable objectives provides direction and motivation, helping to alleviate financial stress.

Example 1: A family sets a short-term goal to save $1,000 for holiday expenses within six months by trimming dining-out expenses by $200 per month.

Example 2: A young professional targets paying off a $5,000 credit card balance within 18 months by dedicating $280 monthly, boosting their confidence as balances decline.

Summary: Setting and achieving realistic goals creates a sense of accomplishment and reduces the overwhelm of financial uncertainty.

Key Takeaways from All Sections:

1. Financial anxiety thrives in uncertainty. Clarity through tracking and planning dismantles fear.
2. Building safety nets like emergency funds and enhancing financial literacy reduce vulnerabilities.
3. Mindfulness and expert guidance empower individuals to face challenges with composure.
4. Realistic, actionable goals pave the way to sustained financial confidence and well-being.

By implementing these strategies and drawing insights from the examples, you can tackle financial anxiety, improving both your financial and mental health.

How To Create A Comprehensive Budget

Creating a comprehensive budget is a fundamental step toward achieving financial stability and reaching your financial goals. By systematically tracking your income and expenses, you can make informed decisions about your spending and savings. Here's a step-by-step guide to help you develop an effective budget:

1. Determine Your Net Income

Your net income is the amount you take home after taxes and other deductions. This figure serves as the foundation of your budget, as it represents the actual funds available for allocation.

Example: If your annual salary is $60,000, your monthly gross income is $5,000. After accounting for taxes and deductions totaling $1,200, your net monthly income is $3,800.

2. Track Your Expenses

Identify and record all your expenditures to understand where your money is going. Categorize them into fixed and variable expenses:

- **Fixed Expenses:** Regular payments that remain constant each month, such as rent or mortgage, car payments, and insurance premiums.

    Example: A monthly rent of $1,200 is a fixed expense.

- **Variable Expenses:** Payments that fluctuate monthly, including groceries, entertainment, and utilities.

    Example: Grocery bills that vary between $300 and $400 each month are variable expenses.

3. Set Financial Goals

Define clear short-term and long-term financial objectives to guide your budgeting process. This will help you prioritize your spending and savings efforts.

Example: A short-term goal might be saving $1,000 for an emergency fund within six months, while a long-term goal could be saving for a down payment on a house over five years.

4. Choose a Budgeting Method

Select a budgeting approach that aligns with your financial habits and goals. Common methods include:

- **50/30/20 Rule:** Allocate 50% of your income to needs, 30% to wants, and 20% to savings or debt repayment.

    Example: With a net income of $3,800, you would allocate $1,900 to needs, $1,140 to wants, and $760 to savings or debt repayment.

- **Zero-Based Budget:** Assign every dollar a specific purpose, ensuring your income minus expenses equals zero.

Example: If your net income is $3,800, you might allocate $1,200 to rent, $400 to groceries, $300 to utilities, $200 to entertainment, and so on, until every dollar is accounted for.

5. Monitor and Adjust Your Budget

Regularly review your budget to ensure it reflects your current financial situation and goals. Make adjustments as necessary to accommodate changes in income, expenses, or objectives.

Example: If you receive a salary increase, decide how to allocate the additional income—perhaps increasing your savings contributions or paying down debt faster.

6. Utilize Budgeting Tools

Leverage tools like spreadsheets, budgeting apps, or financial journals to track your income and expenses consistently. These tools can provide insights into your spending patterns and help you stay on track.

Example: Using a budgeting app, you can categorize expenses, set spending limits, and receive alerts when you're nearing those limits.

Summary

By following these steps, you can create a comprehensive budget that provides clarity on your financial situation, helps you manage your spending, and guides you toward achieving your financial goals. Regular monitoring and flexibility to adjust your budget as circumstances change are key to maintaining financial health.

Interactive Questions and Sample Answers

Creating a comprehensive budget is essential for achieving financial stability and reaching your financial goals. To assist you in this process, here are 10 interactive questions designed to guide you through each step of budgeting:

1. **What is your total monthly net income after taxes and deductions?**

   - Example Answer: $3,800

2. Can you list all your fixed monthly expenses and their amounts?

   - Example Answer: *Rent: $1,200; Car Payment: $300; Insurance: $150

3. What are your variable monthly expenses, and how much do you typically spend on each?

   - Example Answer: Groceries: $350; Entertainment: $200; Utilities: $100

4. What are your short-term financial goals (e.g., saving for a vacation) and long-term goals (e.g., retirement)

   - Example Answer: Short-term: Save $1,000 for a vacation in 6 months; Long-term: Save $20,000 for a home down payment in 5 years

5. Which budgeting method aligns with your financial habits: the 50/30/20 rule or a zero-based budget?

   - Example Answer: The 50/30/20 rule or a zero-based

6. How do you plan to allocate your income according to your chosen budgeting method?

   - Example Answer: Needs: $1,900; Wants: $1,140; Savings/Debt Repayment: $760

7. What tools or apps will you use to track your income and expenses consistently?

   - Example Answer: Mint app for tracking expenses and a Google Sheets spreadsheet for budgeting

8. How often will you review and adjust your budget to reflect changes in your financial situation?

   - Example Answer: Monthly, at the end of each month

9. In case of a salary increase or unexpected expense, how will you adjust your budget allocations?

   - Example Answer: Allocate additional income to increase savings and pay off debt; reduce discretionary spending to cover unexpected expenses

10. What strategies will you implement to ensure you adhere to your budget and financial goals?

   - Example Answer: Set up automatic transfers to savings accounts and use budgeting app alerts to monitor spending

By thoughtfully answering these questions, you can create a personalized and effective budget that aligns with your financial objectives and lifestyle.

Conclusion

Financial uncertainty often leads to significant stress and anxiety, adversely affecting mental health and overall well-being. The American Psychological Association identifies financial stress as a prevalent source of anxiety, impacting individuals' mental health.

Examples Illustrating the Impact of Financial Anxiety on Mental Health

1. **Increased Psychological Distress:**

   - Example: Individuals with greater financial worries exhibit higher levels of psychological distress, including symptoms of anxiety and depression.

2. **Development of Maladaptive Coping Mechanisms:**

   - Example: Some individuals may turn to compulsive behaviors, such as excessive spending or gambling, as a way to cope with financial stress, leading to further financial strain and mental health challenges.

These examples demonstrate how financial anxiety can lead to significant mental health challenges, including increased psychological distress and the development of maladaptive coping mechanisms. Addressing financial stress is crucial for maintaining mental well-being and preventing the escalation of mental health issues.

chapter 2: "Budgeting Isn't About Restriction;
It's About Empowerment."

Chapter 2: Budgeting Isn't About Restriction; It's About Empowerment

Budgeting is often misunderstood as a practice of limitation, but in reality, it's a means of empowerment. By giving every dollar a purpose, you create a roadmap that prioritizes what truly matters to you, ensuring your financial actions align with your values and goals. This chapter dives into six key components of value-based budgeting, enriched with relatable examples and actionable insights.

1. Understanding Budgeting as Empowerment

Budgeting isn't about saying "no" to everything—it's about choosing what you say "yes" to. It allows you to intentionally allocate resources to reflect your values and priorities, fostering a sense of control over your financial life.

Example 1: Emily, a passionate artist, used to feel overwhelmed by her unpredictable spending. By creating a budget, she allocated $200 monthly for art supplies while cutting back on dining out. This shift gave her the freedom to pursue her passion without guilt.

Example 2: Michael, a single parent, prioritized his children's education. His budget redirected $100 from streaming subscriptions toward a college savings fund, bringing peace of mind for their future.

Summary: Understanding that budgeting is about empowerment transforms it from a chore into a tool of intention. By focusing on your goals and values, you can make proactive choices that bring you closer to the life you desire.

2. Identifying Personal Values

Your values are the foundation of an empowering budget. Reflecting on what matters most—whether it's family, health, career, or experiences—helps you allocate resources in a way that resonates deeply with your purpose.

Example 1: Sarah values her physical and mental health. She dedicates $150 each month to yoga classes and therapy sessions, reinforcing her commitment to self-care.

Example 2: Ryan, an environmental enthusiast, adjusted his grocery budget to support local farmers and sustainable products, even if they were slightly more expensive.

Summary: Identifying values ensures that your spending reflects what's meaningful to you. This alignment brings clarity and satisfaction, making it easier to stick to your financial plan.

3. Aligning Spending with Values

Once values are defined, align your spending to reflect them. This alignment may require reallocation from less important areas to those that hold more significance.

Example 1: Julia loves to travel but used to overspend on clothes. She redirected her shopping budget toward a travel fund, enabling her to take a dream vacation every year.

Example 2: Marcus values his community. By shifting $50 from luxury coffee runs to monthly donations for a local food bank, he felt more connected to his neighborhood.

Summary: Aligning spending with values ensures that every dollar contributes to your personal vision. This approach minimizes regret and maximizes fulfillment.

4. Setting Financial Goals

Goals provide direction and motivation, giving your budget a clear purpose. Short-term goals (like paying off a credit card) and long-term goals (like buying a home) guide your financial decisions.

Example 1: Olivia set a goal to save $5,000 in a year for a down payment. By cutting unnecessary expenses, she managed to save $420 monthly and achieved her target early.

Example 2: James wanted to retire early. He adjusted his budget to increase retirement contributions, prioritizing his goal over luxury expenses.

Summary: Setting financial goals aligns your daily actions with your long-term aspirations, ensuring your budget isn't just about surviving but thriving.

5. Monitoring and Adjusting Your Budget

Life is dynamic, and your budget should be, too. Regular reviews help you adapt to changes in income, expenses, or priorities.

Example 1: Lisa received a bonus at work and used it to boost her vacation fund while paying off a small loan. Regularly reviewing her budget allowed her to adjust without guilt.

Example 2: After an unexpected medical bill, Adam reallocated funds from his entertainment budget to cover the expense while staying on track with his goals.

Summary: Monitoring and adjusting your budget ensures it remains a practical and effective tool for your changing needs, allowing you to maintain control without feeling constrained.

6. Overcoming Challenges

Budgeting can be challenging when faced with societal pressures or unplanned expenses. Staying committed requires focus on the bigger picture—your values and goals.

Example 1. Rachel was tempted to buy a designer bag during a sale. Reminding herself of her travel goal helped her resist the purchase and feel proud of her decision.

Example 2. Ethan faced peer pressure to join expensive outings but set a limit on entertainment spending. He suggested alternative activities, maintaining social connections without overspending.

Summary: Challenges will arise, but staying focused on your values empowers you to make choices you won't regret. Every decision strengthens your resolve and brings you closer to your goals.

What You've Learned

Budgeting isn't a constraint; it's a tool that empowers you to live intentionally. By aligning your spending with your values, setting clear goals, and adapting as needed, you create a financial plan that supports your vision for life. This intentional approach reduces stress, fosters confidence, and paves the way for a more fulfilling financial journey. Through consistent effort and reflection, you can transform budgeting from a task into a liberating practice.

Interactive Questions and Sample Answers

1. What are your top three financial priorities, and how does your current spending reflect them?

Sample Answer: My top financial priorities are saving for retirement, maintaining health, and traveling. Currently, I contribute 15% of my income to a retirement fund, allocate funds for a gym membership and healthy groceries, and set aside a portion of my income for future travel plans.

2. How do you differentiate between essential and non-essential expenses in your budget?

Sample Answer: Essential expenses include rent, utilities, groceries, and insurance. Non-essential expenses cover dining out, entertainment, and subscriptions. I prioritize essentials to ensure my basic needs are met before allocating funds to discretionary spending.

3. Can you identify areas where you might be overspending? How can you adjust your budget to address this?

Sample Answer: I tend to overspend on dining out. To address this, I plan to set a monthly limit for restaurant expenses and focus on meal planning to encourage cooking at home.

4. What strategies do you use to ensure you live within your means?

Sample Answer: I track my expenses meticulously, adhere to a budget that aligns with my income, and avoid using credit for non-essential purchases to prevent accumulating debt.

5. How do you plan for unexpected expenses or emergencies?

Sample Answer: I maintain an emergency fund equivalent to six months of living expenses to cover unforeseen costs without disrupting my financial stability.

6. In what ways does your budget support your long-term financial goals?

Sample Answer: My budget allocates specific amounts toward retirement savings, a home down payment fund, and a travel fund, ensuring consistent progress toward these objectives.

7. How do you adjust your budget when your income changes?

Sample Answer: If my income increases, I proportionally increase contributions to savings and investments. If it decreases, I reassess and reduce discretionary spending to maintain financial balance.

8. What tools or methods do you use to track your spending and stay within your budget?

Sample Answer: I use a budgeting app that categorizes expenses and provides real-time updates, helping me monitor spending and adhere to my budget.

9. How do you ensure that your spending habits align with your personal values?

Sample Answer: I regularly review my expenses to confirm they support my priorities, such as sustainability and health, and adjust eliminate spending that doesn't align with these values.

10. What steps do you take to avoid impulse purchases that could disrupt your budget?

Sample Answer: I implement a 24-hour rule for non-essential purchases, allowing time to assess their necessity and alignment with my financial goals before committing.

By engaging with these questions, you can gain deeper insights into your financial behaviors and make informed decisions that empower you to achieve your financial aspirations.

Building Your Budget from the Ground Up

Budgeting is often perceived as a restrictive practice, but it serves as a powerful tool for financial empowerment. By intentionally allocating funds to specific categories, you ensure that your spending aligns with your personal priorities and values, enabling informed financial decisions and reducing stress.

Allocating Funds to Specific Categories: Examples

1. Housing Expenses:
 - Example: Allocating 30% of your monthly income to cover rent or mortgage payments ensures that housing costs remain manageable and do not impede other financial goals.

2. Savings and Investments:
 - Example: Designating 20% of your income to savings accounts, retirement funds, or other investments helps build financial security and prepares for future needs.

3. Debt Repayment:
 - Example: Allocating 15% of your income to pay off credit card balances or student loans can systematically reduce debt and improve credit health.

4. Transportation:
 - Example: Setting aside 10% of your income for car payments, fuel, insurance, or public transportation ensures that mobility expenses are covered without financial strain.

5. Groceries and Dining:
 - Example: Allocating 15% of your income to food-related expenses allows for balanced spending between essential groceries and occasional dining out.

6. Entertainment and Leisure:
 - Example: Designating 5% of your income for hobbies, movies, or other leisure activities ensures enjoyment without compromising essential expenses.

7. Healthcare:

- Example: Setting aside 5% of your income for medical expenses, including insurance premiums and out-of-pocket costs, prepares you for health-related needs.

8. Emergency Fund:
   - Example: Allocating a portion of your income to build an emergency fund provides a financial cushion for unexpected expenses, reducing reliance on credit.

9. Education and Personal Development:
   - Example: Designating funds for courses, books, or workshops supports continuous learning and personal growth.

10. Miscellaneous Expenses:
   - Example: Allocating a small percentage of your income for unforeseen or irregular expenses ensures flexibility in your budget.

By thoughtfully distributing your income across these categories, you create a comprehensive financial plan that reflects your priorities and supports your goals. This intentional approach to budgeting transforms it from a restrictive practice into an empowering tool that fosters financial well-being and peace of mind.

Interactive Questions and Sample Answers

Building a budget from the ground up is a crucial step toward achieving financial stability and aligning your spending with your personal priorities and values. By intentionally allocating funds to specific categories, you can make informed financial decisions and reduce stress. Here are 10 questions with sample answers to guide you through this process:

1. What is your total monthly net income after taxes and deductions?

   Sample Answer: My total monthly net income is $3,800.

2. Can you list your fixed monthly expenses and their amounts?

   Sample Answer: Yes, my fixed expenses include:
   - Rent: $1,200
   - Car Payment: $300
   - Insurance Premiums: $150

3. What are your variable monthly expenses, and how much do you typically spend on each?

   Sample Answer: My variable expenses are:
   - Groceries: $350
   - Entertainment: $200
   - Utilities: $100

4. Have you set specific financial goals, both short-term and long-term?

   Sample Answer: Yes, my short-term goal is to save $1,000 for an emergency fund within six months, and my long-term goal is to save $20,000 for a home down payment over five years.

5. Which budgeting method do you prefer to use, such as the 50/30/20 rule or a zero-based budget?

   Sample Answer: I prefer the 50/30/20 rule, allocating 50% of my income to needs, 30% to wants, and 20% to savings or debt repayment.

6. How do you plan to allocate your income according to your chosen budgeting method?

   Sample Answer: Following the 50/30/20 rule:
   - Needs (50%): $1,900
   - Wants (30%): $1,140
   - Savings/Debt Repayment (20%): $760

7. What tools or methods do you use to track your income and expenses?

   Sample Answer: I use a budgeting app to categorize and monitor my expenses, and I maintain a spreadsheet for detailed tracking.

8. How often do you review and adjust your budget to ensure it aligns with your financial goals?

   Sample Answer: I review my budget monthly to make necessary adjustments based on any changes in income or expenses.

9. How do you handle unexpected expenses or changes in income?

Sample Answer: I maintain an emergency fund to cover unexpected expenses and adjust my discretionary spending to accommodate changes in income.

10. What strategies do you employ to ensure you adhere to your budget?

Sample Answer: I set up automatic transfers to my savings account and use spending alerts from my budgeting app to stay within my budget limits.

By thoughtfully addressing these questions, you can build a comprehensive budget that reflects your financial priorities and supports your goals, transforming budgeting into an empowering tool for financial well-being. Categorizing your expenses is a fundamental step in effective budgeting, as it provides clarity on where your money is going and helps identify areas for adjustment. Here's how you can categorize your expenses:

1. Identify Major Expense Categories

Start by dividing your expenses into broad categories. Common categories include:

-**Housing:** Rent or mortgage payments, property taxes, homeowners insurance, maintenance, and repairs.
-**Utilities:** Electricity, gas, water, sewer, trash services, internet, and phone bills.
-**Transportation:** Car payments, fuel, insurance, public transportation fares, maintenance, and repairs.
- **Food:** Groceries, dining out, and snacks.
- **Insurance:** Health, dental, vision, life, and disability insurance premiums.
- **Healthcare:** Medical expenses, prescriptions, and over-the-counter medications.
- **Debt Repayment:** Credit card payments, student loans, personal loans, and other debts.
- **Savings and Investments:** Emergency fund contributions, retirement accounts, and other savings.
- Personal Spending Clothing, entertainment, hobbies, and personal care items.
- Miscellaneous: Gifts, donations, and other irregular expenses.

2. Use Subcategories for Detailed Tracking

For more precise tracking, break down major categories into subcategories. For example:

- **Housing:**
  - Rent/Mortgage
  - Property Taxes
  - Homeowners Insurance
  - Maintenance and Repairs
- **Transportation:**
  - Car Payment
  - Fuel
  - Insurance
  - Public Transit
  - Maintenance and Repairs

3. Track Your Spending

Record your expenses regularly to monitor spending patterns. Utilize budgeting tools or apps that automatically categorize expenses based on transactions. Review and adjust categories as needed to ensure they align with your financial goals.

By systematically categorizing your expenses, you gain a clearer understanding of your financial habits, enabling you to make informed decisions and maintain control over your finances.

Budgeting Strategies

Implementing proven budgeting strategies is essential for achieving financial stability and ensuring your spending aligns with your financial goals. Here are some effective budgeting methods to consider:

1. 50/30/20 Budget

This method allocates your after-tax income into three categories:

- Needs (50%): Essential expenses such as housing, utilities, groceries, and transportation.
- Wants (30%): Non-essential expenses like dining out, entertainment, and hobbies.
- Savings and Debt Repayment (20%): Allocating funds towards savings, investments, and paying off debts.

This approach provides a balanced framework for managing expenses while prioritizing savings.

2. Zero-Based Budget

In this method, every dollar of income is assigned a specific purpose, ensuring your income minus expenses equals zero. This requires detailed tracking of all expenditures and can help identify unnecessary spending.

3. Envelope System

This cash-based strategy involves allocating cash amounts to categorized envelopes (e.g., groceries, entertainment) for each spending category. Once the cash is spent, no further spending is allowed in that category, promoting disciplined spending habits.

4. Pay-Yourself-First Budget

Also known as reverse budgeting, this method prioritizes savings by allocating a predetermined portion of income to savings or investments before addressing other expenses. The remaining funds are used for necessities and discretionary spending.

5. Continuous Budgeting

This approach involves preparing budgets for future periods and revising them regularly based on actual spending and income, ensuring flexibility and responsiveness to financial changes.

6. Performance-Based Budgeting

Commonly used in organizational settings, this method allocates funds based on the relationship between funding levels and expected results, focusing on achieving specific objectives.

7. Activity-Based Budgeting

This approach allocates costs to specific activities, helping identify and eliminate unnecessary expenses by understanding the true cost of operations.

8. Priority-Based Budgeting

This method involves ranking expenditures based on their importance and aligning spending with strategic priorities, ensuring that funds are directed towards the most critical areas.

9. Incremental Budgeting

This traditional approach adjusts previous budgets by a certain percentage to account for changes, making it simple but potentially overlooking the need for more significant reallocations.

10. Line-Item Budgeting

This method lists individual expenses, providing detailed control over spending but may lack flexibility and a focus on overall objectives.

Selecting the right budgeting strategy depends on your financial goals, spending habits, and personal preferences. Regularly reviewing and adjusting your budget can help maintain financial health and achieve your objectives.

Interactive Questions and Sample Answers

Implementing effective budgeting strategies is crucial for achieving financial stability and ensuring your spending aligns with your financial goals. Here are 10 questions with sample answers to help you understand and apply various budgeting methods:

1. What is the 50/30/20 budgeting rule, and how can it be applied?

Sample Answer: The 50/30/20 rule allocates 50% of after-tax income to needs (essentials like housing and groceries), 30% to wants (non-essentials like entertainment), and 20% to savings or debt repayment. For example, with a monthly net income of $3,000, you would allocate $1,500 to needs, $900 to wants, and $600 to savings or debt repayment.

2. How does the zero-based budgeting method work?

Sample Answer: Zero-based budgeting involves assigning every dollar of income to a specific expense or savings category, ensuring that total income minus total expenses equals zero. This method requires detailed tracking of all expenditures to identify and eliminate unnecessary spending.

3. Can you explain the envelope system and its benefits?

Sample Answer: The envelope system is a cash-based strategy where you allocate cash amounts to categorized envelopes for each spending category (e.g., groceries, entertainment). Once the cash in an envelope is spent, no further spending is allowed in that category, promoting disciplined spending habits and preventing overspending.

4. What is the 'pay-yourself-first' budgeting method?

Sample Answer: Also known as reverse budgeting, this method prioritizes savings by allocating a predetermined portion of income to savings or investments before addressing other expenses. The remaining funds are used for necessities and discretionary spending, ensuring that saving is a priority.

5. How does activity-based budgeting differ from traditional budgeting methods?

Sample Answer: Activity-based budgeting allocates costs to specific activities, helping identify and eliminate unnecessary expenses by understanding the true cost of operations. Unlike traditional budgeting, which may adjust previous budgets by a certain percentage, activity-based budgeting focuses on the costs of activities that drive expenses.

6. What is incremental budgeting, and what are its potential drawbacks?

Sample Answer: Incremental budgeting adjusts previous budgets by a certain percentage to account for changes, making it simple but potentially overlooking the need for more significant reallocations. This approach may perpetuate past inefficiencies and does not encourage the evaluation of existing expenditures.

7. How does performance-based budgeting enhance financial planning

Sample Answer: Performance-based budgeting allocates funds based on the relationship between funding levels and expected results, focusing on achieving specific objectives. This method emphasizes outcomes and aligns resources with organizational goals, enhancing accountability and effectiveness.

8. What is priority-based budgeting, and how does it function?

Sample Answer: Priority-based budgeting involves ranking expenditures based on their importance and aligning spending with strategic priorities, ensuring that funds are directed towards the most critical areas. This approach helps organizations focus resources on high-priority programs and services.

9. Can you describe the line-item budgeting method?

Sample Answer: Line-item budgeting lists individual expenses, providing detailed control over spending but may lack flexibility and a focus on overall objectives. This traditional approach categorizes expenditures by items or classes, making it straightforward but potentially rigid.

10. How can continuous budgeting benefit financial management?

Sample Answer: Continuous budgeting involves preparing budgets for future periods and revising them regularly based on actual spending and income, ensuring flexibility and responsiveness to financial changes. This ongoing process allows for timely adjustments and more accurate financial planning.

By understanding and applying these budgeting strategies, you can select the method that best aligns with your financial goals and spending habits, leading to improved financial management and stability.

Conclusion

Budgeting is often perceived as a restrictive practice, but in reality, it serves as a powerful tool for financial empowerment. By intentionally allocating funds to specific categories, you ensure that your spending aligns with your personal priorities and values, enabling informed financial decisions and reducing stress.

For example, if you value health and wellness, you might allocate a portion of your budget to a gym membership or nutritious groceries. Conversely, if travel is a priority, you could set aside funds regularly to build a travel fund. This intentional allocation allows you to spend money on what truly matters to you, transforming budgeting from a restrictive task into an empowering practice that supports your goals and enhances your overall well-being.

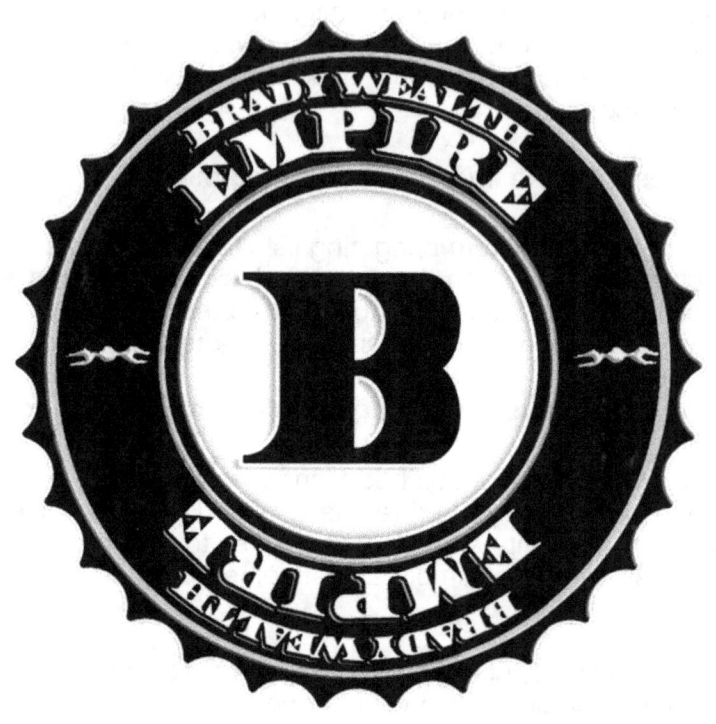

Chapter 3: "Feeling the Weight of Uncertainty Lift as You Track Your Income and Expenses."

Chapter 3: Feeling the Weight of Uncertainty Lift as You Track Your Income and Expenses

Initiating a budget by meticulously tracking your income and expenses is a pivotal step toward achieving financial clarity and control. This process, though initially daunting, empowers you to make informed decisions about your financial future.

1. Identifying Income Sources

Begin by listing all sources of income, including salaries, freelance payments, rental income, or investment returns. This comprehensive overview ensures you account for every dollar earned.

Example 1: If you receive a monthly salary of $3,000 and earn an additional $500 from freelance work, your total monthly income is $3,500.

Example 2: An individual with a part-time job earning $1,200 monthly and a side business generating $800 would have a combined income of $2,000 per month.

Summary: Identifying all income sources provides a clear picture of your financial inflows, which is essential for effective budgeting. By accounting for every dollar earned, you can allocate funds appropriately and avoid overspending.

2. Categorizing Expenses

Divide your expenses into two main categories:

- **Fixed Expenses:** Regular payments that remain constant each month, such as rent or mortgage, car payments, and insurance premiums.

    Example 1: A monthly rent of $1,200 is a fixed expense.

    Example 2: A car loan payment of $300 per month is another fixed expense.

- **Variable Expenses:** Payments that fluctuate monthly, including groceries, entertainment, and utilities.

    Example 1: Grocery bills that vary between $300 and $400 each month are variable expenses.

Example 2: Utility bills that range from $100 to $150 monthly also fall into this category.

Summary: Categorizing expenses into fixed and variable helps in understanding spending patterns and identifying areas where adjustments can be made. This distinction is crucial for creating a realistic budget that accommodates both consistent and fluctuating costs.

3. Recording Transactions

Utilize tools like spreadsheets, budgeting apps, or financial journals to log every transaction. Consistency in recording expenditures and income is crucial for accurate tracking.

Example 1: Using a budgeting app, you record a $50 dining expense immediately after payment, ensuring real-time tracking.

Example 2: Maintaining a financial journal where you note down a $100 grocery purchase helps in keeping a manual record.

Summary: Recording transactions diligently ensures that no expense or income is overlooked, providing a comprehensive view of your financial activities. This practice aids in maintaining financial discipline and accountability.

4. Analyzing Spending Patterns

Review your recorded data to identify spending habits and areas where you can reduce expenses. This analysis helps in making informed financial decisions.

Example 1: Noticing that you spend $200 monthly on subscriptions, you decide to cancel unused services, saving $50 per month.

Example 2: Realizing that dining out costs $300 monthly, you opt to cook more at home, aiming to cut this expense by half.

Summary: Analyzing spending patterns allows you to pinpoint unnecessary expenditures and reallocate funds toward more meaningful financial goals. This proactive approach fosters better financial management.

5. Setting Financial Goals

Define clear short-term and long-term financial objectives, such as building an emergency fund, paying off debt, or saving for a major purchase. Align your budget to facilitate these goals.

Example 1: Aiming to save $5,000 for an emergency fund within a year, you allocate $417 monthly toward this goal.

Example 2: Planning to pay off a $2,400 credit card debt in 12 months, you set aside $200 each month for repayment.

Summary: Setting specific financial goals provides direction and motivation, enabling you to tailor your budget to achieve these objectives systematically. This alignment ensures that your financial activities are purpose-driven.

6. Regular Review and Adjustment

Periodically assess your budget to ensure it reflects your current financial situation and goals. Adjust allocations as necessary to accommodate changes in income, expenses, or objectives.

Example 1: After a salary increase of $500 per month, you choose to increase your monthly savings by $300 and allocate $200 for leisure activities.

Example 2: Facing higher utility bills during winter, you adjust your budget by reducing discretionary spending to cover the increased costs.

Summary: Regularly reviewing and adjusting your budget ensures its relevance and effectiveness, allowing you to respond proactively to financial changes and maintain control over your financial trajectory.

By diligently tracking your income and expenses, you lift the weight of uncertainty, paving the way for financial stability and empowerment. This structured approach enables you to make informed decisions, avoid unnecessary debt, and work confidently toward your financial goals.

Steps to Track Income and Expenses

1. Gather Financial Documents: Collect pay stubs, bank statements, bills, and receipts to have a comprehensive view of your financial activities.

2. Record Income: List all sources of income, noting the amounts and frequencies (e.g., monthly salary, quarterly dividends).

3. List Expenses: Document all expenditures, categorizing them into fixed and variable expenses.

4. Choose a Tracking Method:
   - Manual Tracking: Use a notebook or spreadsheet to log transactions.
   - Budgeting Apps: Utilize applications that sync with your bank accounts to automatically track spending.
   - Envelope System: Allocate cash for different spending categories into designated envelopes to control spending.

5. Review and Analyze: Regularly assess your spending patterns to identify areas where you can reduce expenses and increase savings.

Example

Consider Jane, who earns a monthly salary of $3,500. After tracking her expenses for a month, she discovers the following:

- Fixed Expenses:
  - Rent: $1,200
  - Car Payment: $300
  - Insurance: $150

- Variable Expenses:
  - Groceries: $400
  - Dining Out: $250
  - Entertainment: $150
  - Utilities: $200
  - Miscellaneous: $200

Total Expenses: $2,850

By subtracting her total expenses from her income, Jane realizes she has a surplus of $650 each month. She decides to allocate this surplus toward her savings and paying off debt, thereby enhancing her financial stability.

Interactive Questions and Sample Answers

1. What are your total monthly income and expenses?
   - Sample Answer: My total monthly income is $4,000, and my expenses amount to $3,200.

2. Which expenses are fixed, and which are variable?
   - Sample Answer: Fixed expenses include rent and car payments; variable expenses encompass groceries and entertainment.

3. Are there any expenses you can reduce or eliminate?
   - Sample Answer: I can reduce dining out expenses by cooking at home more often.

4. How much are you saving each month?
   - Sample Answer: I am currently saving $300 each month.

5. Do your spending habits align with your financial goals?
   - Sample Answer: Not entirely; I need to cut back on unnecessary purchases to save more.

6. What tools or methods are you using to track your finances?
   - Sample Answer: I use a budgeting app that syncs with my bank accounts for automatic tracking.

7. Have you set a budget for discretionary spending?
   - Sample Answer: Yes, I allocate $200 monthly for entertainment and dining out.

8. How do you plan to handle unexpected expenses?
   - Sample Answer: I have an emergency fund with three months' worth of expenses to cover unforeseen costs.

9. What are your short-term and long-term financial goals?
   - Sample Answer: Short-term: Pay off credit card debt. Long-term: Save for a down payment on a house.

10. How often do you review and adjust your budget?
   - Sample Answer: I review my budget monthly and make adjustments as needed.

By diligently tracking your income and expenses, you gain valuable insights into your financial habits, enabling you to make informed decisions and work toward your financial objectives with confidence.

Meticulously tracking your income and expenses is a fundamental practice that empowers you to make informed decisions about your financial future. By maintaining detailed records, you gain insights into your spending habits, identify areas for improvement, and set realistic financial goals. This process can be broken down into six key parts, each contributing to enhanced financial management.

1. Comprehensive Income Assessment

Begin by identifying all sources of income, including primary employment, freelance work, rental income, and investment returns. A thorough understanding of your total income establishes the foundation for effective budgeting.

Example 1: An individual earns a monthly salary of $4,000 and receives $500 from freelance projects, resulting in a total monthly income of $4,500.

Example 2: A person has a part-time job earning $2,000 monthly and gains $300 from dividends, totaling $2,300 in monthly income.

Summary: Accurately assessing all income streams ensures that you have a clear picture of your financial inflows, which is essential for creating a realistic budget and making informed spending decisions.

2. Detailed Expense Categorization

Classify your expenses into categories such as housing, utilities, groceries, transportation, entertainment, and savings. This detailed breakdown helps in understanding where your money is allocated.

Example 1: Monthly expenses include $1,200 for rent, $150 for utilities, $400 for groceries, $200 for transportation, $100 for entertainment, and $500 for savings.

Example 2: Expenses are categorized as $800 for mortgage, $100 for utilities, $300 for groceries, $150 for transportation, $50 for entertainment, and $300 for savings.

Summary: Categorizing expenses provides clarity on spending patterns, enabling you to identify areas where adjustments can be made to align with financial goals.

3. Consistent Transaction Recording

Utilize tools such as spreadsheets, budgeting apps, or financial journals to record every financial transaction. Consistency in tracking ensures accuracy in your financial overview.

Example 1: Using a budgeting app, you log a $60 dining expense immediately after payment, ensuring real-time tracking.

Example 2: Maintaining a spreadsheet, you record a $120 grocery purchase, keeping an up-to-date account of expenses.

Summary: Consistent transaction recording prevents oversight of expenditures, providing a comprehensive view of your financial activities and aiding in maintaining financial discipline.

4. Analysis of Spending Habits

Regularly review your recorded data to identify spending trends and pinpoint areas where expenses can be reduced or optimized.

Example 1: Observing a monthly expenditure of $250 on dining out, you decide to cook more at home, aiming to reduce this amount to $150.

Example 2: Noticing a $100 monthly spend on unused subscriptions, you cancel them, reallocating funds to savings.

Summary: Analyzing spending habits allows for the identification of unnecessary expenses, enabling reallocation of resources toward more significant financial objectives.

5. Strategic Financial Planning

Set short-term and long-term financial goals, such as building an emergency fund, purchasing a home, or planning for retirement. Develop a budget that supports these objectives.

Example 1: To save $6,000 for an emergency fund within a year, allocate $500 monthly toward this goal.

Example 2: Planning to buy a car in two years with a $10,000 down payment, set aside $417 monthly.

Summary: Strategic financial planning ensures that your budgeting efforts are purposeful, directing resources toward achieving specific financial milestones.

6. Regular Budget Evaluation and Adjustment

Periodically assess your budget to ensure it reflects current financial circumstances and goals, making necessary adjustments.

Example 1: After receiving a $600 monthly raise, you increase retirement contributions by $300 and allocate $300 for leisure activities.

Example 2: Facing increased utility costs during winter, you reduce discretionary spending to accommodate the higher bills.

Summary: Regular evaluation and adjustment of your budget maintain its effectiveness, allowing you to adapt to financial changes and stay on track toward your goals.

By meticulously tracking income and expenses through these six steps, you gain control over your financial situation, enabling informed decisions that pave the way for a secure financial future.

Bonuses & Unexpected Income

Unexpected income—such as bonuses, gifts, or windfalls—can be a pleasant surprise. Effectively categorizing this income within your budget is essential for maintaining financial clarity and making informed decisions. Here's how to approach it:

1. Create a Separate Income Category

Establish a distinct category in your budget labeled "Unexpected Income" or "Windfalls." This allows you to track these funds separately from your regular income streams, providing a clear picture of your financial inflows.

2. Allocate Funds Intentionally

Once categorized, decide how to utilize the unexpected income in alignment with your financial goals:

- **Debt Repayment:** If you have outstanding debts, consider allocating a portion of the unexpected income toward paying them down.

- **Emergency Fund:** Bolstering your emergency savings can provide a financial cushion for unforeseen expenses.

- **Investments:** Investing can help grow your wealth over time.

- **Personal Enjoyment:** It's reasonable to allocate a small portion for discretionary spending, such as dining out or leisure activities.

3. Update Your Budget

Reflect the unexpected income and its allocation in your budget. This ensures your financial plan remains accurate and up-to-date, allowing for better tracking and management of your resources.

Example Scenario:

Suppose you receive a $1,000 bonus. You might allocate it as follows:

- $500 to credit card debt repayment
- $300 to your emergency fund
- $150 to investment accounts
- $50 for a celebratory dinner

By categorizing and allocating unexpected income thoughtfully, you can enhance your financial stability and progress toward your financial objectives.

Interactive Questions and Sample Answers

1. **Why is it important to track all sources of income, and how can missing even a small income source impact your budget?**

    Sample Answer: Tracking all income ensures accuracy in budgeting. Missing a source like $200 from side gigs can lead to underestimating resources, making it harder to allocate funds efficiently.

2. **What tools or methods do you prefer for categorizing expenses, and why?**

    Sample Answer: I prefer budgeting apps like Mint because they automatically categorize expenses, saving time and reducing errors compared to manual spreadsheets.

3. What do you do if your variable expenses, like groceries, consistently exceed your budget?

Sample Answer: I review receipts to identify unnecessary purchases and set a weekly spending limit to stay within my budget.

4. How can consistent transaction recording prevent financial surprises at the end of the month

Sample Answer: Recording transactions daily keeps me aware of my spending, preventing oversights like exceeding my dining-out budget by $100.

5. What trends would you look for when analyzing your spending habits, and how would you adjust?

Sample Answer: If I notice $300 monthly on coffee shops, I could cut back by brewing coffee at home, reallocating $200 toward savings.

6. How do you decide on short-term versus long-term financial goals, and how does your budget reflect this?

Sample Answer: Short-term goals like saving $1,000 for a vacation are prioritized with a dedicated savings category, while long-term goals like retirement involve consistent investments.

7. What adjustments would you make to your budget after an unexpected income increase?

Sample Answer: If I receive a $500 bonus, I might allocate $200 to savings, $150 for debt repayment, and $150 for leisure.

8. How can unused subscriptions drain your budget, and what steps do you take to address them?

Sample Answer: Unused subscriptions can waste $50–$100 monthly. I audit my accounts quarterly and cancel services I no longer use.

9. What steps do you take to ensure your financial goals remain aligned with life changes, like moving to a new city?

Sample Answer: I review and adjust my budget to reflect higher rent costs and plan for new expenses like public transport or furniture.

10. How often should you review your budget, and what indicators suggest it's time for an adjustment?

   Sample Answer: I review my budget monthly, but major changes like a salary raise or unexpected medical bills prompt immediate revisions.

Maintaining detailed financial records is crucial for understanding your spending habits and achieving financial stability. Here are six key practices, each illustrated with two examples, to help you gain insight into your financial behaviors:

1. Regular Expense Tracking

- **Example 1:** Sarah uses a budgeting app to record every purchase she makes, from her morning coffee to utility bills. By reviewing her monthly spending reports, she realizes she's spending $150 monthly on dining out, prompting her to cook more at home.

- **Example 2:** John keeps a daily spending journal, noting each expense manually. After a month, he identifies a pattern of impulsive online shopping, leading him to set stricter limits on discretionary spending.

Summary: Consistently tracking expenses, whether digitally or manually, reveals spending patterns and highlights areas where adjustments can be made to align with financial goals.

2. Categorizing Expenses

- **Example 1:** Emily divides her expenses into categories such as housing, transportation, food, and entertainment. This categorization shows that entertainment consumes a larger portion of her budget than anticipated, prompting a reevaluation.

- **Example 2:** Michael uses color-coded spreadsheets to categorize his expenses. He discovers that his utility costs are higher than average, leading him to implement energy-saving measures.

Summary: Organizing expenses into specific categories provides clarity on spending distribution, helping identify areas for potential savings.

3. Reviewing Bank and Credit Card Statements

- **Example 1:** Lisa reviews her bank statements monthly to ensure all transactions are accurate. She notices multiple small fees from her bank and decides to switch to a fee-free account.

- **Example 2:** Tom examines his credit card statements and finds subscriptions he no longer uses. Canceling these services saves him $50 per month.

Summary: Regularly reviewing financial statements helps detect unnecessary charges and ensures spending aligns with personal priorities.

4. Setting and Monitoring Budgets

- **Example 1:** Anna sets a monthly budget for groceries and tracks her spending against it. Staying within budget allows her to allocate surplus funds to her savings.

- **Example 2:** David establishes a budget for transportation expenses. Monitoring his spending helps him decide to use public transit more often to reduce costs.

Summary: Establishing budgets for different expense categories and monitoring adherence promotes disciplined spending and financial planning.

5. Analyzing Spending Trends Over Time

- **Example 1:** Rachel compares her quarterly spending reports and notices a gradual increase in utility bills. Investigating further, she identifies and fixes a water leak, reducing future expenses.

- **Example 2:** Mark analyzes his annual spending and sees a spike in holiday expenses. Planning ahead, he sets aside a monthly amount to prepare for seasonal costs.

Summary: Examining spending trends over extended periods uncovers patterns that inform proactive financial decisions.

6. Retaining Receipts and Invoices

- **Example 1:** Jessica keeps digital copies of all her receipts. This practice helps her track warranty periods and return items within allowed timeframes, preventing unnecessary losses.

- **Example 2:** Kevin organizes his invoices for freelance work, ensuring accurate income tracking and simplifying tax preparation.

Summary: Maintaining receipts and invoices supports accurate record-keeping, aids in dispute resolution, and facilitates efficient tax filing.

By implementing these practices, individuals can gain a comprehensive understanding of their spending habits, identify areas for improvement, and make informed decisions to enhance their financial well-being.

Interactive Questions and Sample Answers

1. How do you currently track your daily expenses?

    - **Sample Answer:** I use a budgeting app that syncs with my bank accounts to automatically log purchases. For cash transactions, I enter them manually at the end of the day.

2. What categories do you use to organize your expenses, and how do they help you identify spending patterns?

    - **Sample Answer:** I divide my expenses into categories like housing, transportation, food, entertainment, and savings. This helps me see that I've been spending too much on entertainment and can redirect those funds to savings.

3. When was the last time you reviewed your bank or credit card statements, and what did you learn?

    - **Sample Answer:** reviewed my credit card statement last week and found I was still paying for an unused subscription. I canceled it and saved $15 per month.

4. Do you use a specific budgeting method? How do you monitor adherence to it?

    - **Sample Answer:** I follow the 50/30/20 rule, allocating 50% of my income to needs, 30% to wants, and 20% to savings. I review my spending weekly to ensure I stay within those percentages.

5. Have you identified any trends in your spending over time? If so, how have you addressed them?

- **Sample Answer:** I noticed an increase in my grocery bills over the past three months. I started meal planning and buying in bulk to save on costs.

6. Do you keep physical or digital copies of your receipts and invoices? Why?

- **Sample Answer:** I keep digital copies of all receipts using a scanning app. It helps me track expenses for warranty claims and simplifies tax preparation.

7. How do you handle unexpected expenses that arise?

- **Sample Answer** I use funds from my emergency savings account, which I built by setting aside 10% of my income each month.

8. What steps have you taken to reduce unnecessary spending after analyzing your financial records?

- **Sample Answer:** After tracking my expenses, I realized I was spending $100 monthly on unused memberships. I canceled them and redirected that money to my travel savings.

9. How often do you review and adjust your budget?
- Sample Answer: I review my budget at the end of every month to assess any changes in income or expenses. I make adjustments as needed to stay aligned with my financial goals.

10. What tools or systems have you found most effective for managing your financial records?

- Sample Answer: I use a combination of a budgeting app for daily tracking and a spreadsheet for monthly reviews. This system provides both real-time updates and a big-picture overview.

Benefits of Answering These Questions

These interactive questions encourage reflection on financial behaviors, reveal areas for improvement, and highlight effective practices for maintaining detailed records. By addressing these points, individuals can gain-better control over their finances and make more informed decisions about their spending habits.

Chapter 4: "The Raw, Visceral Satisfaction of Knowing Exactly Where Every Penny Goes—and Why It Matters."

Chapter 4: The Raw, Visceral Satisfaction of Knowing Exactly Where Every Penny Goes—and Why It Matters

Achieving financial clarity and control begins with a comprehensive understanding of your financial transactions. This awareness not only fosters a sense of accomplishment but also ensures that your spending habits align with your personal values and long-term objectives, which is essential for attaining financial stability and success.

1. The Importance of Tracking Every Penny

Monitoring your expenses allows you to identify spending patterns, curb impulsive purchases, and make informed financial decisions. By diligently tracking where your money goes, you can pinpoint areas where you might be overspending and adjust accordingly. This practice not only aids in adhering to a budget but also fosters a sense of responsibility and control over your financial well-being.

Example 1: An individual tracks their daily expenditures and discovers they spend $150 monthly on coffee shop visits. Recognizing this, they decide to brew coffee at home, reducing this expense to $30 per month.

Example 2: By reviewing their spending, another person realizes they are paying for multiple streaming services they rarely use, totaling $60 monthly. They choose to cancel the unused subscriptions, saving that amount each month.

Summary: These examples illustrate how tracking every expense can reveal unnecessary spending, enabling you to make adjustments that align with your financial goals. By identifying and eliminating superfluous expenses, you can redirect funds toward more meaningful purposes, enhancing financial stability.

2. Aligning Spending with Personal Values

Intentional spending involves directing your financial resources toward what truly matters to you. By aligning your expenditures with your core values, you ensure that your money supports your priorities, leading to greater fulfillment and purpose in your financial decisions. This approach encourages mindful consumption and helps in avoiding expenditures that don't contribute to your overall well-being.

Example 1: If environmental sustainability is a core value, you might choose to support businesses with strong environmental policies or reduce consumption of single-use plastics. This could involve purchasing eco-friendly products or supporting local farmers' markets.

Example 2: Valuing family time could lead you to allocate more funds toward family vacations or activities that strengthen familial bonds, ensuring your spending reflects this priority. This might mean investing in experiences like camping trips or family game nights.

Summary: These scenarios demonstrate how aligning spending with personal values can lead to more intentional and satisfying financial choices. By focusing on what truly matters, you can eliminate spending that doesn't serve your priorities, leading to a more purposeful allocation of resources.

3. Setting Financial Goals

Establishing clear financial goals provides direction and motivation for your spending habits. Whether it's saving for a home, reducing debt, or building an emergency fund, having specific objectives helps in creating a roadmap for your financial journey.

Example 1: A person sets a goal to save $10,000 for a down payment on a house within two years. They determine they need to save approximately $417 per month to reach this target.

Example 2: Another individual aims to pay off $5,000 in credit card debt over 18 months. They plan to allocate around $278 monthly toward debt repayment.

Summary: These examples highlight the importance of setting specific, measurable financial goals. By defining clear objectives, you can create actionable plans to achieve them, fostering financial discipline and progress.

4. Creating a Budget

A budget serves as a financial blueprint, outlining your income and expenses to ensure you live within your means. It helps in prioritizing spending, avoiding debt, and allocating funds toward your financial goals.

Example 1: An individual earns $3,000 monthly and allocates funds as follows: $1,200 for rent, $300 for groceries, $200 for utilities, $100 for transportation, $200 for entertainment, and $500 for savings.

Example 2: Another person with a $4,000 monthly income budgets $1,500 for mortgage, $400 for groceries, $300 for utilities, $200 for transportation, $300 for dining out, and $800 for retirement savings.

Summary: These budgeting examples illustrate how allocating specific amounts to various expenses ensures that all financial obligations are met while also contributing to savings and goals. A well-structured budget promotes financial stability and prevents overspending.

5. Regular Financial Review

Consistently reviewing your financial situation allows you to assess progress toward your goals and make necessary adjustments. Regular check-ins help in adapting to changes in income, expenses, or priorities.

Example 1: A person reviews their budget monthly and notices an increase in utility bills during winter. They adjust by reducing discretionary spending to accommodate the higher costs.

Example 2: Another individual receives a salary increase and decides to allocate the additional income toward their retirement fund, enhancing their long-term financial security.

Summary: Regular financial reviews enable proactive management of your finances, allowing you to respond effectively to changes and stay on track with your objectives. This practice ensures that your financial plan remains relevant and effective.

6. Seeking Professional Guidance

Consulting with financial advisors or utilizing financial planning resources can provide personalized strategies and insights. Professional guidance helps in navigating complex financial decisions and optimizing your financial plan.

Example 1 An individual nearing retirement consults a financial advisor to develop a retirement strategy that aligns with their goals and risk tolerance.

Example 2: A young professional seeks advice on investment options to grow their wealth, receiving tailored recommendations based on their financial situation.

Summary: Engaging with financial professionals offers expertise and personalized advice, enhancing your financial decision-making and planning. This support can be instrumental in achieving financial success and confidence.

By meticulously tracking your income and expenses, aligning spending with personal values, setting clear financial goals, creating a structured budget, conducting regular financial reviews, and seeking professional guidance, you can attain a profound sense of control and satisfaction over your financial life. These practices empower you to make informed decisions, reduce financial stress, and work toward lasting financial stability and success.

Aligning your spending with your personal values involves directing your financial resources toward what truly matters to you, ensuring that your expenditures reflect your beliefs and priorities. This intentional approach to spending fosters a sense of fulfillment and purpose in your financial decisions.

Steps to Align Spending with Personal Values:

1. Identify Your Core Values:

   - Reflect on what is most important to you, such as family, health, environmental sustainability, or financial security. Understanding these values is the first step toward aligning your spending accordingly.

2. Assess Current Spending Habits:

   - Review your recent expenditures to determine if they support or contradict your identified values. This assessment can reveal discrepancies between your spending and your priorities.

3. Make Intentional Spending Decisions:

   - Before making purchases, consider whether they align with your core values. This mindfulness helps in avoiding impulsive buys that don't contribute to your overall well-being.

4. Create a Values-Based Budget:

- Develop a budget that allocates funds toward areas that reflect your values, ensuring that your financial plan supports what matters most to you.

Examples:

- **Environmental Sustainability:**

  - If you value sustainability, you might choose to support businesses with strong environmental policies or reduce consumption of single-use plastics.

- **Family Prioritization:**

  - Valuing family time could lead you to allocate more funds toward family vacations or activities that strengthen familial bonds, ensuring your spending reflects this priority.

Benefits:

Aligning your spending with your values fosters a sense of purpose and contentment. Financial decisions become reflections of what truly matters to you, leading to healthier financial habits.

By consciously directing your financial resources toward what you value most, you not only achieve greater satisfaction but also ensure that your spending habits contribute positively to your overall well-being and long-term goals.

Interactive Questions and Sample Answers

1. **What are your top three personal values?**

    - **Sample Answer:** Family, environmental sustainability, and personal growth.

2. **How does your current spending reflect these values?**

    - **Sample Answer*:** I allocate funds for family vacations, purchase eco-friendly products, and invest in educational courses.

3. **Can you identify expenses that don't align with your values?**

- **Sample Answer:** Frequent dining out doesn't align with my health goals, and shopping for fast fashion contradicts my commitment to sustainability.

4. What steps can you take to reduce spending in areas misaligned with your values?

- **Sample Answer:** Plan meals to minimize eating out and choose sustainable clothing brands.

5. How can you reallocate funds to better support your priorities?

- **Sample Answer:** Redirect savings from reduced dining out to family activities and personal development courses.

6. Do you have a system in place to track your expenses?

- **Sample Answer:** Yes, I use a budgeting app to monitor my spending and ensure it aligns with my values.

7. How often do you review your spending habits?

- **Sample Answer:** I review my expenses monthly to assess alignment with my financial goals and values.

8. What challenges do you face in aligning your spending with your values?

- **Sample Answer:** Impulse purchases and social pressures sometimes lead to spending that doesn't reflect my priorities.

9. How do you plan to overcome these challenges?

- **Sample Answer:** Implementing a waiting period before non-essential purchases and setting clear financial goals to stay focused.

10. What benefits do you anticipate from aligning your spending with your values?**

- **Sample Answer:** Greater financial satisfaction, reduced stress, and a stronger sense of purpose in my financial decisions.

By meticulously tracking your expenses and ensuring they reflect your personal values, you pave the way toward financial stability and a more fulfilling life. This intentional approach to spending transforms your financial habits into a true reflection of what matters most to you.

Achieving financial clarity involves a comprehensive understanding of your financial transactions and long-term objectives. Here are six key components to guide you, each illustrated with two examples:

1. Tracking Income and Expenses

Example 1: Sarah uses a budgeting app to record her monthly income and categorize expenses such as rent, groceries, and entertainment. This practice helps her identify spending patterns and areas where she can cut back.

Example 2: John maintains a spreadsheet detailing his daily expenditures. Reviewing it weekly allows him to adjust his spending habits and ensure he stays within his budget.

Summary: Regular tracking of income and expenses provides insight into spending behaviors, enabling informed financial decisions and effective budgeting.

2. Setting SMART Financial Goals

Example 1: Emily aims to save $10,000 for a home down payment within two years. She sets a monthly savings target of $417, aligning with the SMART criteria (Specific, Measurable, Achievable, Relevant, Time-bound).

Example 2. Michael plans to pay off $5,000 in credit card debt over 18 months by allocating $278 monthly, ensuring his goal is realistic and time-bound.

Summary: Establishing SMART financial goals offers clear direction and measurable milestones, facilitating progress tracking and financial discipline.

3. Creating and Following a Budget

Example 1: Lisa adopts the 50/30/20 budgeting rule, allocating 50% of her income to needs, 30% to wants, and 20% to savings and debt repayment. This structure balances her financial obligations and personal desires.

Example 2: Mark uses a zero-based budget, assigning every dollar a purpose, ensuring his income minus expenses equals zero, which helps him control his spending.

Summary: Implementing a structured budget aligns spending with financial goals, promoting responsible money management.

4. Building an Emergency Fund

Example 1: Anna sets up an automatic transfer of $200 monthly into a high-yield savings account, aiming to accumulate three months' worth of living expenses for emergencies.

Example 2: Tom directs his annual tax refund into an emergency fund, gradually building a financial cushion for unexpected events.

Summary: An emergency fund provides financial security, reducing reliance on credit during unforeseen circumstances.

5. Monitoring and Improving Credit Health

Example 1: Rachel regularly reviews her credit report for errors and pays her bills on time to maintain a good credit score, facilitating favorable loan terms.

Example 2: James reduces his credit card balances to improve his credit utilization ratio, positively impacting his credit score.

Summary: Maintaining good credit health is essential for accessing financial opportunities and securing favorable interest rates.

6. Planning for Retirement

Example 1: Karen contributes 15% of her salary to her employer's 401(k) plan, taking advantage of employer matching contributions to build her retirement fund.

Example 2: David opens an Individual Retirement Account (IRA) and sets up automatic monthly contributions, ensuring consistent retirement savings.

Summary: Early and consistent retirement planning ensures financial stability in later years, leveraging compound interest and employer benefits.

By integrating these practices, you can achieve financial clarity, effectively manage transactions, and work towards long-term financial objectives.

Interactive Questions and Sample Answers

1. How do you currently track your income and expenses?

   Sample Answer: I use a budgeting app to record all my income sources and categorize expenses, which helps me monitor my spending habits and identify areas for improvement.

2. Can you provide an example of a SMART financial goal you've set?

   Sample Answer: I aim to save $5,000 for an emergency fund within 12 months by setting aside $417 each month, ensuring the goal is Specific, Measurable, Achievable, Relevant, and Time-bound.

3. What budgeting method do you find most effective, and why?

   Sample Answer: The 50/30/20 rule works best for me, as it allocates 50% of income to needs, 30% to wants, and 20% to savings or debt repayment, providing a balanced approach to managing finances.

4. How have you built or how do you plan to build your emergency fund?

   * **Answer:** I set up an automatic monthly transfer of $200 into a high-yield savings account to gradually build an emergency fund covering three months' living expenses.

5. What steps do you take to monitor and improve your credit health?

   Sample Answer: I regularly check my credit reports for accuracy, pay bills on time, and keep credit card balances low to maintain a healthy credit score.

6. How are you planning for retirement?

Sample Answer: I contribute 15% of my salary to my employer's 401(k) plan and take advantage of employer matching contributions to build my retirement savings.

7. How do you differentiate between needs and wants in your budgeting process?

Sample Answer: I categorize essential expenses like housing and groceries as needs, while discretionary spending like dining out and entertainment falls under wants, helping me prioritize my spending.

8. What challenges have you faced in sticking to your budget, and how have you overcome them?

Sample Answer: Impulse purchases were a challenge, but implementing a 24-hour rule before making non-essential buys has helped me reduce unnecessary spending.

9. How do you ensure your financial goals are realistic and achievable?

Sample Answer: I assess my income, expenses, and financial commitments to set goals that are attainable within a specific timeframe, ensuring they align with my overall financial plan.

10. What strategies do you use to stay motivated towards achieving your long-term financial objectives?

Sample Answer: I break down long-term goals into smaller milestones, celebrate achievements along the way, and regularly review my progress to stay motivated and on track.

Engaging with these questions can help you reflect on your financial practices and identify areas for improvement, leading to better financial clarity and success.

Reducing debt requires a strategic approach

Reducing debt requires a strategic approach and disciplined financial habits. Here are several effective strategies to help you manage and eliminate debt:

1. **Create a Detailed Budget:**

   - **Track Income and Expenses:** Document all sources of income and categorize expenses to understand your spending patterns. This clarity helps identify areas where you can cut back and allocate more funds toward debt repayment.

   - **Set Spending Limits:** Establish limits for discretionary spending categories to ensure you live within your means and prevent additional debt accumulation.

2. **Prioritize Debt Repayment Methods:**

   - **Debt Snowball Method** Focus on paying off the smallest debts first while making minimum payments on larger ones. This approach builds momentum as each debt is eliminated.

   - **Debt Avalanche Method:** Prioritize debts with the highest interest rates to minimize the total interest paid over time, leading to quicker debt reduction.

3. **Consolidate Debts:**

   - **Debt Consolidation Loans:** Combine multiple debts into a single loan with a lower interest rate, simplifying payments and potentially reducing the overall interest paid.

   - **Balance Transfer Credit Cards:** Transfer high-interest credit card balances to a card offering a lower interest rate or an introductory 0% APR period to save on interest.

4. **Increase Income Streams:**

   - **Side Hustles:** Engage in part-time work or freelance opportunities to generate additional income dedicated to debt repayment.

   - **Sell Unused Items:** Declutter and sell items you no longer need to raise extra funds for paying down debts.

5. **Negotiate with Creditors:**

   - **Lower Interest Rates:** Contact creditors to request reduced interest rates, which can lower monthly payments and total interest paid.

- **Payment Plans:** Work with creditors to establish manageable payment plans that fit your budget.

6. Seek Professional Assistance:

   - **Credit Counseling:** Consult with certified credit counselors who can provide personalized advice and help create a debt management plan.

   - **Debt Management Plans (DMPs):** Enroll in a DMP through a reputable agency to consolidate payments and potentially secure lower interest rates.

7. Adopt Frugal Living Practices:

   - **Reduce Unnecessary Expenses:** Cut back on non-essential spending, such as dining out or subscription services, to free up funds for debt repayment.

   - **Use Cash or Debit Cards:** Avoid using credit cards to prevent accumulating new debt; instead, use cash or debit cards to control spending.

8. Build an Emergency Fund:
   - Save for Emergencies: Allocate a portion of your income to an emergency fund to cover unexpected expenses, reducing the need to incur additional debt.

Implementing these strategies can help you systematically reduce debt and achieve financial stability. Consistency and commitment to these practices are key to successful debt elimination.

Effectively tracking expenses

Effectively tracking expenses is crucial for financial management, and various tools can assist in this process:

1. Budgeting Applications: Apps like YNAB (You Need A Budget) and Mint allow users to link bank accounts, categorize transactions, and monitor spending against budgets. These platforms often provide visualizations to help users understand their financial habits.

2. Spreadsheets: Utilizing programs like Microsoft Excel or Google Sheets enables individuals to create customized expense tracking systems. This method offers flexibility in categorizing expenses and tailoring the tracking process to specific needs.

3. Expense Management Software: Tools such as QuickBooks and Expensify are designed for both personal and business expense tracking, offering features like receipt scanning, mileage tracking, and integration with accounting systems.

4. Banking Services: Many banks provide online portals and mobile apps that automatically categorize transactions, offering insights into spending patterns directly from one's bank account.

5. Manual Tracking: Maintaining a physical ledger or notebook to record daily expenses can be effective for those who prefer a hands-on approach, promoting mindfulness about spending habits.

Selecting the appropriate tool depends on individual preferences, financial goals, and the desired level of detail in tracking expenses.

Budgeting is a fundamental tool

Budgeting is a fundamental tool for effective financial management, offering numerous benefits that enhance both short-term and long-term financial well-being. Key advantages include:

1. Control Over Finances: Budgeting allows individuals to plan and monitor their spending, ensuring that expenses do not exceed income. This control helps prevent debt accumulation and promotes financial stability.

2,Achievement of Financial Goals: By allocating resources towards specific objectives, such as saving for a home or paying off debt, budgeting facilitates the attainment of both short-term and long-term financial goals.

3. Preparation for Emergencies: Incorporating savings into a budget enables the creation of an emergency fund, providing a financial cushion for unexpected expenses like medical bills or car repairs.

4. Reduction of Financial Stress: Having a clear plan for income and expenses reduces uncertainty and anxiety related to financial matters, leading to improved mental well-being.

5. Improved Spending Habits: Budgeting encourages mindful spending by distinguishing between needs and wants, helping individuals make informed decisions and avoid impulsive purchases.

6. Enhanced Savings By identifying and eliminating unnecessary expenditures, budgeting frees up resources that can be directed towards savings and investments, contributing to wealth accumulation.

7. Better Financial Organization: Maintaining a budget organizes financial information, making it easier to track bills, due dates, and financial obligations, thereby avoiding late fees and penalties.

In summary, budgeting serves as a roadmap for financial success, enabling individuals to manage their money effectively, prepare for unforeseen events, and work towards their financial aspirations with confidence.

Advanced savings strategies

Advanced savings strategies can significantly enhance your financial growth and stability. Here are some effective methods to consider:

1. Maximize Retirement Contributions: Contribute the maximum allowable amount to retirement accounts such as 401(k)s or IRAs. This not only prepares you for retirement but also offers tax advantages. For instance, high earners can utilize strategies like the "mega-backdoor Roth" to contribute up to $70,000 to their 401(k) in 2025.

2. Automate Savings: Set up automatic transfers from your checking account to a high-yield savings account or investment account. This ensures consistent saving without manual effort, allowing your funds to grow over time.

3. Utilize Tax-Advantaged Accounts: Take advantage of Health Savings Accounts (HSAs) and Flexible Spending Accounts (FSAs) to save for medical expenses with pre-tax dollars, reducing your taxable income.

4. Implement the 'Pay Yourself First' Strategy: Prioritize saving by allocating a portion of your income to savings before addressing other expenses. This approach ensures that saving is a primary focus in your financial planning.

5. Practice Goal-Based Investing: Align your investment strategies with specific financial goals, such as purchasing a home or funding education. This method helps in creating a tailored investment plan that meets your objectives.

6. Adopt the FIRE Approach: The Financial Independence, Retire Early (FIRE) movement emphasizes aggressive saving and investing to achieve early retirement. This involves maximizing savings rates and investing wisely to generate sufficient passive income.

7. Leverage Employer Matching Contributions: If your employer offers matching contributions to retirement plans, contribute at least enough to receive the full match. This is essentially an immediate return on your investment.

8. Diversify Investments: Spread your investments across various asset classes to mitigate risk and enhance potential returns. A diversified portfolio can better withstand market volatility.

9. Engage in Tax-Loss Harvesting: Offset capital gains by selling investments at a loss, thereby reducing your taxable income. This strategy can optimize your tax situation.

10. Regularly Review and Adjust Your Financial Plan: Periodically assess your financial goals and investment performance to ensure alignment with your objectives. Adjust your strategies as needed to stay on track.

Implementing these advanced savings strategies requires careful planning and, in some cases, consultation with financial professionals to tailor them to your specific circumstances. By doing so, you can effectively work towards achieving your long-term financial goals.

Implementing advanced savings strategies

Implementing advanced savings strategies can significantly enhance your financial growth and stability. To deepen your understanding, consider the following interactive questions with sample answers:

1. How can maximizing retirement contributions benefit your financial future?

   Sample Answer: Contributing the maximum allowable amount to retirement accounts like a 401(k) or IRA not only prepares you for retirement but also offers tax advantages, such as reducing taxable income and allowing investments to grow tax-deferred.

2. What are the advantages of automating your savings?

Sample Answer: Automating savings ensures consistent contributions to your savings or investment accounts without manual effort, promoting disciplined saving habits and leveraging compound interest over time.

3. How do Health Savings Accounts (HSAs) and Flexible Spending Accounts (FSAs) provide tax benefits?

Sample Answer: HSAs and FSAs allow you to save for medical expenses with pre-tax dollars, reducing your taxable income and providing a tax-efficient way to cover healthcare costs.

4. What does the 'Pay Yourself First' strategy entail, and why is it effective?

Sample Answer: The 'Pay Yourself First' strategy involves allocating a portion of your income to savings before addressing other expenses, ensuring that saving is prioritized and integrated into your financial planning.

5. Can you explain goal-based investing and its importance?

Sample Answer: Goal-based investing aligns your investment strategies with specific financial objectives, such as buying a home or funding education, helping create a tailored plan to meet your unique goals.

6. What is the FIRE movement, and how does it aim to achieve financial independence?

Sample Answer: The Financial Independence, Retire Early (FIRE) movement emphasizes aggressive saving and investing to generate sufficient passive income, enabling individuals to retire earlier than traditional retirement ages.

7. Why is it beneficial to contribute enough to receive your employer's matching contributions in retirement plans?

Sample Answer: Employer matching contributions are essentially an immediate return on your investment, effectively doubling your contribution up to the match limit and accelerating your retirement savings.

8. How does diversifying your investments mitigate risk?

Sample Answer: Diversifying investments across various asset classes spreads risk, reducing the impact of any single investment's poor performance on your overall portfolio.

9. What is tax-loss harvesting, and how can it optimize your tax situation?

Sample Answer: Tax-loss harvesting involves selling investments at a loss to offset capital gains, thereby reducing taxable income and optimizing your tax liabilities.

10. Why is it important to regularly review and adjust your financial plan?

Sample Answer: Regularly reviewing and adjusting your financial plan ensures alignment with your evolving financial goals and market conditions, allowing you to make informed decisions and stay on track.

Engaging with these questions can help you assess your current financial strategies and identify areas for improvement, ultimately enhancing your financial growth and stability.

Chapter 5: "The Rush of Freedom That Comes When You Face the Truth About Your Spending and Decide to Shift Your Priorities."

Chapter 5: The Rush of Freedom That Comes When You Face the Truth About Your Spending and Decide to Shift Your Priorities

Confronting your spending habits can be a liberating experience. Recognizing areas where your expenditures do not align with your goals enables you to make necessary adjustments. This proactive approach facilitates the redirection of resources towards what truly matters to you, fostering a sense of purpose and direction in your financial journey.

1. Self-Assessment of Spending Habits

Begin by conducting a thorough audit of your current expenses. This involves tracking all expenditures to identify patterns and areas where spending may not align with your financial goals. Utilizing budgeting apps or maintaining a detailed spending journal can aid in this process.

Example 1: An individual discovers that a significant portion of their monthly income is spent on dining out. Recognizing this, they decide to prepare meals at home more frequently, thereby reducing unnecessary expenses.

Example 2: Another person realizes they are spending excessively on subscription services they rarely use. By canceling these subscriptions, they free up funds for more important financial goals.

Summary: Conducting a self-assessment of spending habits allows individuals to identify areas where their expenditures may not align with their financial objectives. By recognizing and addressing these discrepancies, they can redirect resources toward more meaningful goals, leading to improved financial well-being.

2. Identifying Misaligned Expenditures

Analyze your spending to pinpoint expenses that do not support your financial objectives. This step requires honesty and may involve confronting uncomfortable truths about habitual spending.

Example 1: A person aiming to save for a home down payment realizes that their frequent online shopping for non-essential items is hindering their savings goal.

Example 2: An individual planning for retirement notices that daily premium coffee purchases are adding up, diverting funds from their retirement savings.

Summary: Identifying misaligned expenditures helps individuals understand how certain spending habits can impede financial progress. By addressing these habits, they can reallocate funds to support their financial objectives more effectively.

3. Setting Clear Financial Goals

Establish specific, measurable, achievable, relevant, and time-bound (SMART) financial goals. Clear objectives provide direction and motivation for adjusting spending habits.

Example 1: Setting a goal to save $5,000 over the next year for an emergency fund by allocating a portion of each paycheck to a dedicated savings account.

Example 2: Planning to pay off $3,000 in credit card debt within 18 months by making consistent monthly payments above the minimum requirement.

Summary: Setting clear financial goals offers a roadmap for financial decision-making. It encourages disciplined spending and saving behaviors aligned with one's long-term objectives.

4. Creating a Realistic Budget

Develop a budget that reflects your income, necessary expenses, and financial goals. Ensure it is realistic to maintain sustainability.

Example 1: Allocating 50% of income to necessities, 30% to discretionary spending, and 20% to savings, adjusting as needed to meet specific goals.

Example 2: Using the envelope method to allocate cash for different spending categories, helping to control discretionary spending.

Summary: Creating a realistic budget serves as a financial blueprint, guiding spending and saving decisions. It ensures that resources are allocated effectively to meet both immediate needs and future goals.

5. Implementing Changes and Monitoring Progress

Make the necessary adjustments to your spending habits and monitor your progress regularly. This may involve using financial tracking tools or setting reminders to review your budget.

Example 1: Using a budgeting app to track daily expenses and ensure adherence to the new spending plan.

Example 2: Setting monthly calendar reminders to review financial statements and assess progress toward goals.

Summary: Implementing changes and monitoring progress fosters accountability and allows for timely adjustments. This proactive approach helps maintain alignment with financial objectives.

6. Reflecting and Adjusting as Necessary

Regularly reflect on your financial journey, celebrating successes and addressing challenges. Be prepared to adjust your budget and goals as circumstances change.

Example 1: After reaching a savings milestone, reassessing financial goals to set new objectives, such as investing or planning for retirement.

Example 2: Adjusting the budget to accommodate a new job with a different salary structure, ensuring continued progress toward financial goals.

Summary: Regular reflection and adjustment ensure that financial plans remain relevant and effective. This flexibility allows individuals to adapt to changing circumstances while staying on track toward their objectives.

By systematically addressing each of these areas, you can align your spending with your financial goals, leading to greater financial freedom and personal fulfillment.
Example: The Daily Coffee Habit

10 Interactive Questions to Assess and Align Your Spending Habits

1. **What are your top three financial goals?**

    - **Sample Answer:** Saving for a home down payment, building an emergency fund, and investing for retirement.

2. **How do you currently track your spending?**

    - **Sample Answer:** I use a budgeting app to monitor my expenses and categorize them accordingly.

3. Can you identify any expenses that do not support your financial goals?

   - **Sample Answer:** Yes, frequent dining out and impulsive online shopping do not align with my goal of saving for a home.

4. What steps can you take to reduce or eliminate these non-essential expenses?

   - **Sample Answer:** I plan to cook more meals at home and set a monthly limit for discretionary online purchases.

5. How do you differentiate between needs and wants in your spending?

   - **Sample Answer:** Needs are essential expenses like rent and groceries, while wants are non-essential items like entertainment subscriptions.

6. Have you set a monthly budget that reflects your financial priorities?

   - **Sample Answer:** Yes, I allocate specific amounts to necessities, savings, and discretionary spending to ensure alignment with my goals.

7. How often do you review and adjust your budget?

   - **Sample Answer:** I review my budget monthly to track progress and make necessary adjustments.

8. What challenges do you face in sticking to your budget, and how can you overcome them?

   - **Sample Answer:** Impulse purchases are a challenge; using a 24-hour rule before buying non-essential items helps mitigate this.

9. How do you plan to monitor your progress toward your financial goals?

   - **Sample Answer:** I set milestones and use my budgeting app to track savings and expenditures related to each goal.

10. In what ways can you reward yourself for adhering to your financial plan without derailing your progress?

    - Sample Answer: I allocate a small portion of my budget for leisure activities as a reward for meeting my savings targets.

By engaging with these questions, you can gain clarity on your spending habits and take actionable steps to align them with your financial aspirations. This alignment not only fosters financial health but also enhances overall well-being by reducing stress and increasing satisfaction.

Confronting your spending habits is essential for aligning your expenditures with your financial goals. By identifying areas where your spending does not support your objectives, you can make necessary adjustments to ensure your financial resources are directed toward what truly matters. Here are six key areas to focus on, each with examples of misaligned spending and strategies for realignment:

1. Dining Out vs. Home-Cooked Meals

- Misaligned Spending: Regularly eating at restaurants or ordering takeout can significantly impact your budget, diverting funds from savings or debt repayment goals.

    Example: Spending $15 on lunch daily amounts to $300 monthly, which could otherwise be allocated toward an emergency fund.

    - Adjustment Strategy: Plan and prepare meals at home to reduce dining expenses. Bringing lunch to work can save a substantial amount over time.

    Example: Preparing lunch at home for $5 per meal saves $200 monthly compared to buying lunch, allowing you to contribute more to your savings.

2. Subscription Services

- Misaligned Spending: Maintaining multiple subscription services that are seldom used can drain financial resources.

    Example: Paying for streaming services, magazines, and gym memberships totaling $100 monthly, despite rarely using them.

- **Adjustment Strategy:** Review and cancel unnecessary subscriptions, retaining only those that provide regular value.

  Example: Canceling unused subscriptions saves $80 monthly, which can be redirected toward paying off credit card debt.

3. Impulse Purchases

  - **Misaligned Spending:** Making unplanned purchases, especially of non-essential items, can derail budgeting efforts.

  Example: Buying clothing or gadgets on a whim, leading to an extra $200 spent monthly.

  - **Adjustment Strategy:** Implement a waiting period before making non-essential purchases to assess necessity.

  Example: Adopting a 30-day rule for non-essential items reduces impulse spending, freeing up funds for investment contributions.

4. Transportation Costs

  - **Misaligned Spending:** Opting for convenience through ride-sharing services or driving instead of using public transportation increases expenses.

  Example: Spending $150 monthly on ride-shares instead of a $60 public transit pass.

  - **Adjustment Strategy:** Utilize cost-effective transportation methods like public transit, biking, or carpooling.

  Example: Switching to a public transit pass saves $90 monthly, which can be allocated to a retirement account.

5. Entertainment Expenses

  - **Misaligned Spending:** Frequent outings to movies, concerts, or events can strain your budget.

  Example: Spending $200 monthly on entertainment while struggling to save for a vacation.

- **Adjustment Strategy:** Seek free or low-cost entertainment alternatives and set a monthly entertainment budget.

   Example: Limiting entertainment spending to $100 monthly allows you to save an additional $100 toward your vacation fund.

6. Utility Usage

- **Misaligned Spending:** High utility bills due to excessive energy consumption can divert funds from other financial goals.

   Example: Leaving lights and appliances on unnecessarily results in a $150 monthly utility bill.

- **Adjustment Strategy:** Implement energy-saving practices to reduce utility costs.

   Example: Using energy-efficient appliances and mindful consumption lowers the utility bill to $100, freeing up $50 monthly for other priorities.

Summary

By scrutinizing your spending habits in areas such as dining, subscriptions, impulse purchases, transportation, entertainment, and utility usage, you can identify expenditures that do not align with your financial goals. Implementing targeted adjustments, like preparing meals at home, canceling unused subscriptions, adopting waiting periods for purchases, utilizing cost-effective transportation, setting entertainment budgets, and conserving energy, enables you to redirect funds toward savings, debt repayment, investments, or other financial objectives. This proactive approach fosters financial discipline and accelerates progress toward achieving your goals.

Adjusting your budget is essential to ensure your spending aligns with your financial goals, especially when circumstances change. Here are some examples of budget adjustments:

1. Reducing Discretionary Spending

- **Example:** If you find that you're overspending on entertainment, consider cutting back on activities like dining out or attending events. Instead, opt for free or low-cost alternatives, such as hosting a movie night at home or exploring local parks.

2. Refinancing Loans

- **Example:** If you're paying high interest rates on loans, refinancing to a lower rate can reduce your monthly payments. This adjustment frees up funds that can be redirected toward savings or other financial goals.

3. Adjusting Savings Contributions

- **Example:** If you receive a salary increase, consider increasing your contributions to retirement accounts or emergency funds. This proactive adjustment helps in building a more secure financial future.

4. Modifying Transportation Expenses

- **Example:** If fuel prices rise, consider using public transportation, carpooling, or biking to work. These changes can significantly reduce transportation costs, allowing you to allocate funds elsewhere.

5. Revising Grocery Budgets

- **Example:** If grocery expenses are higher than planned, try buying in bulk, choosing generic brands, or shopping during sales. These strategies can help lower food costs and keep your budget on track.

6. Updating Utility Usage

- **Example:** Implement energy-saving measures like using energy-efficient appliances or adjusting thermostats to reduce utility bills. Lower utility costs can free up money for other priorities.

Regularly reviewing and adjusting your budget ensures that your spending habits support your financial objectives, helping you stay on track toward achieving your goals.

Identifying spending leaks

Identifying spending leaks—small, often unnoticed expenses that accumulate over time—is crucial for maintaining financial health. By scrutinizing your spending habits, you can pinpoint and address these leaks, ensuring your money is directed toward your financial goals. Here's how to identify and rectify common spending leaks:

1. Track Your Expenses

Maintain a detailed record of all your expenditures, categorizing them to highlight where your money goes. This practice reveals patterns and areas of overspending.

Example: Using a budgeting app, you discover that daily coffee purchases amount to $150 monthly.

2. Review Subscription Services

Regularly assess all active subscriptions to determine their necessity and usage. Cancel those that are underutilized or redundant.

Example: Noticing multiple streaming services, you decide to keep only the one you use frequently, saving $30 per month.

3. Monitor Impulse Purchases

Be mindful of unplanned spending, especially on non-essential items, as these can quickly add up.

Example: Realizing that spontaneous online shopping sprees cost an extra $200 monthly, you implement a 24-hour rule before making such purchases.

4. Evaluate Food Expenses

Assess how much you spend on dining out versus cooking at home. Preparing meals can be more cost-effective and healthier.

Example: By reducing restaurant visits from five times a week to two, you save approximately $150 monthly.

5. Analyze Utility Bills

Examine your utility bills for any unnecessary charges or inefficiencies. Implementing energy-saving measures can reduce costs.

Example: Switching to energy-efficient appliances lowers your electricity bill by $50 per month.

6. Avoid Unnecessary Fees

Be vigilant about bank fees, late payment charges, and ATM fees, which can erode your finances.

Example: Setting up automatic payments prevents late fees, saving you $25 monthly.

7. Limit Convenience Purchases

Frequent purchases of convenience items, like bottled water or snacks, can add up over time.

Example: Bringing a reusable water bottle reduces daily spending on beverages, saving $45 monthly.

8. Reassess Insurance Policies

Periodically review your insurance policies to ensure you're not overpaying for coverage you don't need.

Example: Comparing auto insurance rates leads you to switch providers, saving $200 annually.

9. Plan Grocery Shopping

Unplanned grocery trips can lead to overspending on items you don't need. Creating a shopping list helps control expenses.

Example: Sticking to a weekly grocery list reduces your food bill by $60 per month.

10. Address Lifestyle Inflation

Be cautious of increasing your spending as your income rises, a phenomenon known as lifestyle creep. Maintain a budget that aligns with your financial goals.

Example: After a salary increase, you resist upgrading to a more expensive car, choosing instead to boost your savings.

By diligently monitoring your spending habits and making conscious adjustments, you can effectively plug financial leaks, ensuring your resources are allocated toward achieving your financial objectives.

Interactive Questions with Sample Answers

Identifying and addressing spending leaks—small, often unnoticed expenses that accumulate over time—is crucial for maintaining financial health. To help you pinpoint these leaks, consider the following interactive questions:

1. Do you track all your daily expenses, including small purchases like coffee or snacks?

Example: Recording every expenditure reveals that daily coffee purchases amount to $150 monthly.

2. How many subscription services are you currently paying for, and do you use them all regularly?

Example: Maintaining multiple streaming services but regularly using only one may lead to unnecessary expenses.

3. Do you often make impulse purchases, either online or in-store?

Example: Unplanned online shopping sprees can add an extra $200 to your monthly expenses.

4. How frequently do you dine out or order takeout instead of cooking at home?

Example: Reducing restaurant visits from five times a week to two can save approximately $150 monthly.

5. Have you reviewed your utility bills for any unnecessary charges or inefficiencies?

Example: Implementing energy-saving measures can reduce electricity bills by $50 per month.

6. Are you incurring bank fees, late payment charges, or ATM fees regularly?

Example: Setting up automatic payments can prevent late fees, saving $25 monthly.

7. Do you frequently purchase convenience items like bottled water or snacks?

Example: Bringing a reusable water bottle reduces daily spending on beverages, saving $45 monthly.

8. When was the last time you compared insurance policies to ensure you're not overpaying?

Example: Switching auto insurance providers after comparison can save $200 annually.

9. Do you plan your grocery shopping trips, or do you make unplanned visits that lead to overspending?

Example Sticking to a weekly grocery list can reduce your food bill by $60 per month.

10. Have you noticed an increase in your spending as your income rises, known as lifestyle inflation?

Example: Resisting the urge to upgrade to a more expensive car after a salary increase allows you to boost your savings instead.

By reflecting on these questions and examining your spending habits, you can identify and address financial leaks, ensuring your resources are directed toward achieving your financial objectives.

Chapter 6: "This Is Your First Step to True Financial Freedom."

Chapter 6: This Is Your First Step to True Financial Freedom

Embarking on the journey to financial freedom begins with embracing budgeting as a powerful tool for empowerment. By taking control of your finances, you set the foundation for achieving your financial goals and securing a stable future. Understanding and implementing effective budgeting practices are pivotal steps toward financial empowerment. By shedding light on your financial habits and making informed decisions, you can transform your financial landscape and work towards lasting stability and success.

1. Tracking Income and Expenses

Monitoring all sources of income and categorizing expenses is essential to understand your spending patterns. This practice provides a clear picture of your financial inflows and outflows, enabling you to manage your money wisely.

Example 1: Using a budgeting app, you record your monthly salary of $4,000 and freelance income of $500. You categorize expenses such as rent ($1,200), groceries ($400), and entertainment ($200).

Example 2: In a spreadsheet, you list your income from a part-time job ($2,000) and investment returns ($300). Expenses are categorized into utilities ($150), dining out ($250), and transportation ($100).

Summary: By diligently tracking income and expenses, you gain insight into your financial habits, allowing for informed decisions and effective money management.

2. Setting Financial Goals

Defining short-term and long-term objectives, such as saving for emergencies or paying off debt, provides direction for your financial planning. Clear goals motivate disciplined budgeting and spending.

Example 1: Setting a short-term goal to save $1,000 for an emergency fund within six months by saving approximately $167 monthly.

Example 2: Establishing a long-term goal to pay off $10,000 in student loans over five years by allocating $167 monthly towards debt repayment.

Summary: Setting specific financial goals offers a roadmap for your budgeting efforts, ensuring that your financial activities align with your aspirations.

3. Allocating Funds Appropriately

Distributing income to cover necessities, discretionary spending, and savings ensures that all financial obligations are met while working towards your goals.

Example 1: Applying the 50/30/20 rule: 50% of income ($2,250) for needs, 30% ($1,350) for wants, and 20% ($900) for savings.

Example 2: Using the envelope system, you allocate cash into envelopes labeled for rent, groceries, entertainment, and savings, spending only what's in each envelope.

Summary: Appropriate fund allocation balances immediate needs with future goals, promoting financial stability and progress.

4. Regular Review and Adjustment

Periodically assessing your budget ensures it aligns with your financial goals and allows for necessary adjustments in response to changes in income or expenses.

Example 1: After receiving a raise, you review your budget to increase contributions to your retirement fund.

Example 2: Facing higher utility bills during winter, you adjust discretionary spending to accommodate the increased expenses.

Summary: Regular reviews and adjustments keep your budget relevant and effective, enabling proactive financial management.

5. Utilizing Budgeting Tools

Employing tools like spreadsheets, budgeting apps, or financial journals aids in organizing and monitoring your financial information efficiently.

Example 1: Using a budgeting app that syncs with your bank accounts to automatically categorize transactions and track spending.

Example 2: Maintaining a detailed spreadsheet that lists income and expenses, with charts visualizing spending patterns.

Summary: Utilizing budgeting tools enhances accuracy and provides clarity, simplifying the budgeting process.

6. Seeking Professional Guidance

Consulting financial advisors or utilizing educational resources can provide personalized advice and strategies tailored to your financial situation.

Example 1: Meeting with a financial planner to develop a comprehensive plan for debt repayment and investment.

Example 2: Attending financial literacy workshops to gain knowledge on effective budgeting and saving techniques.

Summary: Professional guidance offers expertise and support, empowering you to make informed financial decisions and achieve your goals.

By embracing these budgeting practices, you illuminate your financial habits and make informed decisions, transforming your financial landscape towards lasting stability and success.

Examples of Budgeting Methods

1. **Zero-Based Budgeting:** Assign every dollar a specific purpose, ensuring income minus expenses equals zero. This method promotes intentional spending and saving.

2. **50/30/20 Rule:** Allocate 50% of income to necessities, 30% to discretionary items, and 20% to savings or debt repayment. This approach balances needs and wants while promoting savings.

3. **Envelope System:** Assign cash amounts to spending categories, placing the cash in designated envelopes. Once an envelope is empty, no more spending occurs in that category, promoting discipline.

Interactive Questions with Sample Answers

1. What is your total monthly income from all sources?

Sample Answer: My total monthly income, including my salary and freelance work, is $4,500.

2. List your fixed monthly expenses (e.g., rent, utilities). What is the total amount?

Sample Answer: My fixed expenses include rent ($1,200), utilities ($150), car payment ($300), and insurance ($200), totaling $1,850.

3. Identify your variable expenses (e.g., groceries, entertainment). How much do you spend on these monthly?

Sample Answer: I spend approximately $400 on groceries, $150 on dining out, $100 on entertainment, and $50 on miscellaneous items, totaling $700.

4. How much do you allocate to savings each month? Is it a fixed amount or a percentage of your income?

Sample Answer: I allocate $500 monthly to savings, which is about 11% of my income.

5. Do you have an emergency fund? If so, how many months of expenses can it cover?

Sample Answer: Yes, my emergency fund can cover three months of expenses.

6. What are your short-term financial goals (within the next year)?

Sample Answer: My short-term goals include paying off a $2,000 credit card debt and saving $3,000 for a vacation.

7. What are your long-term financial goals (5 years or more)?

Sample Answer: Long-term goals include saving for a home down payment and building a retirement fund.

8. How do you track your spending? Do you use any tools or apps?

Sample Answer: I use a budgeting app to categorize and monitor my expenses.

9. **Have you identified areas where you can reduce spending? If so, what are they?**

   Sample Answer: I plan to reduce dining out and limit entertainment expenses to save more.

10. **How often do you review and adjust your budget?**

    Sample Answer: I review my budget monthly to ensure it aligns with my financial goals.

By thoughtfully engaging with these questions, you can gain clarity on your financial situation and ensure that your budgeting practices align with your personal values and aspirations. This self-assessment is a crucial step toward achieving true financial freedom. decisions, you can transform your financial landscape and work towards lasting stability and success.

Setting realistic financial goals is essential for achieving financial stability and success. By following a structured approach, you can establish clear objectives and create a roadmap to attain them. Here's how to set realistic financial goals:

1. **Define Specific Goals**

Clearly articulate what you want to achieve. Specific goals provide direction and a clear target to work towards.

Example: Instead of saying, "I want to save money," specify, "I want to save $5,000 for an emergency fund within the next 12 months."

2. **Ensure Goals Are Measurable**

Quantify your goals to track progress effectively. Measurable goals allow you to assess your advancement and make necessary adjustments.

Example: "I will save $400 each month to reach my $5,000 emergency fund goal in 12 months."

3. **Set Achievable and Realistic Goals**

Assess your financial situation to set goals that are attainable. Consider your income, expenses, and existing obligations to ensure your goals are realistic.

Example: If your monthly discretionary income is $500, aiming to save $400 per month is achievable. However, attempting to save $800 per month may be unrealistic and lead to frustration.

4. Establish Time-Bound Objectives

Assign deadlines to your goals to create a sense of urgency and motivation. Time-bound goals help in maintaining focus and measuring success.

Example: "I aim to pay off my $3,000 credit card debt within 15 months by paying $200 each month."

5. Prioritize Your Goals

Determine which goals are most important and tackle them accordingly. Prioritization ensures that you focus your resources on what matters most.

Example: Prioritizing building an emergency fund before saving for a vacation ensures financial security in case of unexpected expenses.

6. Develop an Action Plan

Outline the steps needed to achieve each goal. An action plan serves as a roadmap, detailing how you'll reach your objectives.

Example: To save $400 monthly, you might cut dining out expenses by $150, reduce entertainment costs by $100, and allocate an extra $150 from a side job.

7. Monitor Progress Regularly

Review your goals periodically to assess progress and make adjustments as needed. Regular monitoring keeps you on track and allows for flexibility.

Example: Set a monthly reminder to review your savings and adjust your budget if necessary to stay aligned with your goals.

By implementing these steps, you can set realistic financial goals that are tailored to your circumstances, paving the way for financial success and peace of mind.

Aligning your financial goals with your income is essential for achieving financial stability and success. Here's how to ensure your goals are in harmony with your earnings:

1. Assess Your Current Financial Situation

- Calculate Your Net Income: Determine your total monthly income after taxes and deductions.

Example: If your gross monthly salary is $4,000 and taxes amount to $800, your net income is $3,200.

- List Monthly Expenses: Document all fixed and variable expenses to understand your spending patterns.

Example: Fixed expenses: rent ($1,200), car payment ($300); Variable expenses: groceries ($400), entertainment ($150).

2. Prioritize Financial Goals

- Categorize Goals by Time Frame:

  - Short-Term Goals: Achievable within a year (e.g., building an emergency fund).

  - Mid-Term Goals: Attainable within 1-5 years (e.g., saving for a car).

  - Long-Term Goals: Require more than 5 years (e.g., retirement savings).

- Align Goals with Income:

  - Ensure that the allocation towards each goal is feasible given your current income and expenses.

Example: If aiming to save $5,000 for a car in two years, you need to save approximately $208 monthly.

3. Create a Realistic Budget

- Allocate Funds:

  - Assign portions of your income to necessities, discretionary spending, and savings.

Example: Using the 50/30/20 rule: 50% for needs ($1,600), 30% for wants ($960), and 20% for savings ($640).

- **Adjust Spending Habits:**

   - Identify areas to reduce expenses to free up funds for your goals.

   Example: Cutting back on dining out can save $100 monthly, which can be redirected to savings.

4. Automate Savings

- **Set Up Automatic Transfers:**

   - Schedule regular transfers to savings accounts to ensure consistent contributions.

   Example: Automate a $200 transfer to your emergency fund each payday.

- **Utilize Employer Programs:**

   - Enroll in automatic retirement contributions, especially if employer matching is available.

   Example: Contribute 5% of your salary to a 401(k) plan, with employer matching.

5. Monitor and Adjust Regularly

- **Review Financial Progress:**

   - Periodically assess your budget and goals to ensure alignment with your income.

   Example: Quarterly reviews to track savings growth and adjust as needed.

- **Adapt to Income Changes:**

   - Modify your budget and goals in response to income increases or decreases.

Example: After a salary raise, increase savings contributions proportionally.

By systematically evaluating your financial situation, setting prioritized and achievable goals, and maintaining flexibility, you can effectively align your financial objectives with your income, paving the way for financial well-being.

Conclusion: Aligning Your Financial Goals with Your Income

Aligning your financial goals with your income is the cornerstone of achieving lasting financial stability and freedom. It begins with a clear understanding of where you are today—your income, expenses, and any debt—and progresses to creating a roadmap that ensures your financial decisions are intentional, purposeful, and in alignment with your true desires.

When your financial goals reflect your actual income, you empower yourself to make informed, realistic decisions that support both your present needs and future aspirations. This approach allows you to live within your means, avoid the stress of financial overwhelm, and steadily work toward the life you dream of.

Remember, the key is not to focus solely on the numbers, but to recognize that your income is a tool to help you live the life you envision. By setting clear goals, breaking them down into manageable steps, and regularly reviewing your progress, you create a feedback loop that keeps you on track. Each small success fuels the next, and soon, you'll see how every decision—from budgeting to saving to investing—moves you closer to financial freedom.

In the end, aligning your goals with your income isn't about restricting yourself; it's about giving yourself the freedom to live intentionally, making choices based on what matters most, and building a secure foundation for a future filled with opportunities. With patience, discipline, and focus, the life you've always dreamed of is not only possible but within reach.

www.ingramcontent.com/pod-product-compliance
Lightning Source LLC
Chambersburg PA
CBHW071418220526
45469CB00004B/1335